رَّحِيم ٱلرَّحْمَـٰنِ ٱللَّهِ بِسْمِ

Bismillah hir rahman nir Raheem

"In the name of Allah, the Entirely Merciful, the Especially Merciful"

بسم الله الرحمن الرحيم

O Allah, guide me among those You have guided, pardon me among those You have pardoned, turn to me in friendship among those on whom You have turned in friendship, and bless me in what You have bestowed, and save me from the evil of what You have decreed. For verily you decree, and none can influence you; and he is not humiliated whom you have befriended, Blessed are You, O Lord, and Exalted.

Your notes:-

"The Opening of the Quran"

Table of Contents

Surah Al Fatiha..4

Summary of Surah Al-Fatiha...5

Surah Al-Fatiha Arabic 7

Surah Al-Fatiha Arabic, English Pronunciation, and Translation.............8

Surah Al-Fatiha English Pronunciation..10

Surah Al-Fatiha English Translation 11

Surah Yaseen...13

Summary of Surah Yaseen...14

Surah Yaseen Arabic...17

Surah Yaseen Arabic, English Pronunciation, and Translation 24

Surah Yaseen English Pronunciation 47

Surah Yaseen English Translation 53

Surah Ar- Rahman 61

Summary of Surah Ar-Rahman...62

Surah Ar-Rahman Arabic 65

Surah Ar-Rahman Arabic, English Pronunciation, and Translation 73

Surah Ar-Rahman English Pronunciation...87

Surah Ar-Rahman English Translation 92

Surah

Al Fatiha

الفاتحة

Surah Al-Fatiha is the first chapter of the Holy Quran, and it holds immense significance and importance in Islam. Here are some reasons why:

It is a fundamental pillar of the prayer: Muslims recite Surah Al-Fatiha in every unit of their five daily prayers. It is considered one of the most essential parts of the prayer, and the prayer is incomplete without its recitation.

It is the Opening of the Quran: Surah Al-Fatiha is also known as the "Opening" because it serves as the opening chapter of the Quran. It sets the tone for the rest of the Quran and provides an introduction to the teachings of Islam.

It is a summary of the Quran: Surah Al-Fatiha contains the essence of the Quran's message, making it a summary of the entire scripture. The chapter teaches Muslims about the oneness of Allah, His mercy, and the importance of seeking His guidance.

It is a means of seeking Allah's guidance: Muslims believe that Surah Al-Fatiha is a powerful prayer that can help them seek Allah's guidance in all aspects of life. It reminds them that Allah is the only source of guidance and that they should always turn to Him for help.

It is a source of blessings: Muslims believe that reciting Surah Al-Fatiha brings numerous blessings and rewards from Allah. They believe that reciting it with sincerity and devotion can help them overcome difficulties and achieve success in this life and the hereafter.

In summary, Surah Al-Fatiha is a crucial chapter of the Quran that serves as the foundation of Islam's teachings. Its significance lies in its role as a fundamental pillar of prayer, a summary of the Quran's message, a means of seeking Allah's guidance, and a source of blessings for Muslims.

Surah Al-Fatiha
الفاتحة

١. بِسْمِ ٱللَّهِ ٱلرَّحْمَـٰنِ ٱلرَّحِيمِ

٢. ٱلْحَمْدُ لِلَّهِ رَبِّ ٱلْعَـٰلَمِينَ

٣. ٱلرَّحْمَـٰنِ ٱلرَّحِيمِ

٤. مَـٰلِكِ يَوْمِ ٱلدِّينِ

٥. إِيَّاكَ نَعْبُدُ وَإِيَّاكَ نَسْتَعِينُ

٦. ٱهْدِنَا ٱلصِّرَٰطَ ٱلْمُسْتَقِيمَ

٧. أَنْعَمْتَ عَلَيْهِمْ غَيْرِ ٱلْمَغْضُوبِ

صِرَٰطَ ٱلَّذِينَ عَلَيْهِمْ وَلَا ٱلضَّآلِّينَ

Surah Al-Fatiha

ٱلرَّحِيمِ ٱلرَّحْمَـٰنِ ٱللَّهِ بِسْمِ

1. Bismillāhi r-raḥmāni r-raḥīm

In the name of God, the Lord of Mercy, the Giver of Mercy!

ٱلْعَـٰلَمِينَ رَبِّ لِلَّهِ ٱلْحَمْدُ

2. Al ḥamdu lillāhi rabbi l-ʿālamīn

Praise belongs to God, Lord of the Worlds,

ٱلرَّحِيمِ ٱلرَّحْمَـٰنِ

3. Ar raḥmāni r-raḥīm

 The Lord of Mercy, the Giver of Mercy,

ٱلدِّينِ يَوْمِ مَـٰلِكِ

4. Māliki yawmi d-dīn

Master of the Day of Judgement.

نَسْتَعِينُ وَإِيَّاكَ نَعْبُدُ إِيَّاكَ

5. Iyyāka na'budu wa iyyāka nasta'īn

It is you we worship; it is you we ask for help.

ٱلْمُسْتَقِيمَ ٱلصِّرَٰطَ ٱهْدِنَا

6. Ihdinā ṣ-ṣirāṭ al-mustaqīm

Guide us to the straight path:

وَلَا عَلَيْهِمْ ٱلْمَغْضُوبِ غَيْرِ عَلَيْهِمْ أَنْعَمْتَ ٱلَّذِينَ صِرَٰطَ ٱلضَّآلِّينَ

7. Ṣirāṭ al-laḏīna an'amta 'alayhim ġayril maġḍūbi 'alayhim walāḍ ḍāllīn

The path of those you have blessed, those who incur no anger and who have not gone astray.

Surah Al-Fatiha
Pronunciation

1. Bismillāhi r-raḥmāni r-raḥīm

2. Al ḥamdu lillāhi rabbi l-'ālamīn

3. Ar raḥmāni r-raḥīm

4. Māliki yawmi d-dīn

5. Iyyāka na'budu wa iyyāka nasta'īn

6. Ihdinā ṣ-ṣirāṭ al-mustaqīm

7. Ṣirāṭ al-laḏīna an'amta 'alayhim ġayril maġḍūbi 'alayhim walāḍ ḍāllīn

Surah Al-Fatiha

Pronunciation

1. In the name of God, the Lord of Mercy, the Giver of Mercy!

2. Praise belongs to God, Lord of the Worlds,

3. The Lord of Mercy, the Giver of Mercy,

4. Master of the Day of Judgement.

5. It is you we worship; it is you we ask for help.

6. Guide us to the straight path:

7. The path of those you have blessed, those who incur no anger and who have not gone astray.

Your notes:-

"The Opening of the Quran"

Surah Yaseen

يٰسٓ

Surah Yaseen

يسٓ

Surah Yaseen (يسٓ) is the 36th chapter of the Qur'an. Also commonly known as Ya-Sin. Only Allah knows the meaning of Ya-Sin.

It consists of 83 short ayats. Our prophet Muhammad (pbuh) - the Messenger of Allah – said, "If anyone recites Ya-Sin [for Allah's pleasure] at the beginning of the day, his needs will be fulfilled."-

Many scholars have said that the reward for reciting Surah Yasin fully once is as much as reading the Holy Qur'an ten times.

Surah Yaseen is the 36th chapter of the Quran, and it holds immense significance and importance in Islam. Here are some reasons why:

It is a Heart of Quran: Prophet Muhammad (peace be upon him) has referred to Surah Yaseen as the "heart of the Quran" due to its profound and central message. It highlights the oneness of Allah and the importance of submitting to His will.

It is a source of blessings: Muslims believe that reciting Surah Yaseen brings numerous blessings and rewards from Allah. They believe that reciting it with sincerity and devotion can help them overcome difficulties, protect them from evil, and earn the mercy of Allah.

It is a means of seeking forgiveness: Surah Yaseen emphasizes the importance of seeking forgiveness from Allah and turning to Him in repentance. Muslims believe that reciting it can help them attain forgiveness and mercy from Allah.

It comforts the dying: Surah Yaseen is often recited at the time of death, as it provides comfort and reassurance to the dying person. Muslims believe that it eases the transition into the afterlife and helps the soul find peace.

It strengthens faith: Surah Yaseen contains powerful messages about the afterlife and the Day of Judgment. It reminds Muslims of the importance of living a righteous life and striving for the hereafter. It strengthens their faith and encourages them to live according to the teachings of Islam.

In summary, Surah Yaseen is a chapter of the Quran that serves as a source of blessings, forgiveness, and comfort for Muslims. Its significance lies in its central message of the oneness of Allah, the importance of seeking forgiveness, and the emphasis on the afterlife. It is a powerful reminder for Muslims to live a righteous life and strive for the hereafter.

Surah Yaseen

يٰسٓ

بِسْمِ ٱللَّهِ ٱلرَّحْمَـٰنِ ٱلرَّحِيمِ

١. يٰسٓ

٢. وَٱلْقُرْءَانِ ٱلْحَكِيمِ

٣. إِنَّكَ لَمِنَ ٱلْمُرْسَلِينَ

٤. عَلَىٰ صِرَٰطٍ مُّسْتَقِيمٍ

٥. تَنزِيلَ ٱلْعَزِيزِ ٱلرَّحِيمِ

٦. لِتُنذِرَ قَوْمًا مَّآ أُنذِرَ ءَابَآؤُهُمْ فَهُمْ غَـٰفِلُونَ

٧. لَقَدْ حَقَّ ٱلْقَوْلُ عَلَىٰ أَكْثَرِهِمْ فَهُمْ لَا يُؤْمِنُونَ

٨. إِنَّا جَعَلْنَا فِىٓ أَعْنَـٰقِهِمْ أَغْلَـٰلًا فَهِىَ إِلَى ٱلْأَذْقَانِ فَهُم مُّقْمَحُونَ

٩. وَجَعَلْنَا مِنۢ بَيْنِ أَيْدِيهِمْ سَدًّا وَمِنْ خَلْفِهِمْ سَدًّا فَأَغْشَيْنَـٰهُمْ فَهُمْ لَا يُبْصِرُونَ

١٠. وَسَوَآءٌ عَلَيْهِمْ ءَأَنذَرْتَهُمْ أَمْ لَمْ تُنذِرْهُمْ لَا يُؤْمِنُونَ

١١. إِنَّمَا تُنذِرُ مَنِ ٱتَّبَعَ ٱلذِّكْرَ وَخَشِىَ ٱلرَّحْمَـٰنَ بِٱلْغَيْبِ فَبَشِّرْهُ بِمَغْفِرَةٍ وَأَجْرٍ كَرِيمٍ

أَحْصَيْنَهُ شَيْءٍ وَكُلَّ وَءَاثَرَهُمْ قَدَّمُوا۟ مَا وَنَكْتُبُ ٱلْمَوْتَىٰ نُحْىِ نَحْنُ إِنَّا

١٢. مُّبِينٍ إِمَامٍ فِى

١٣. ٱلْمُرْسَلُونَ جَآءَهَا إِذْ ٱلْقَرْيَةِ أَصْحَٰبَ مَّثَلًا لَهُم وَٱضْرِبْ

إِلَيْكُم إِنَّآ فَقَالُوا۟ بِثَالِثٍ فَعَزَّزْنَا ٱثْنَيْنِ إِلَيْهِمُ أَرْسَلْنَآ إِذْ

١٤. مُّرْسَلُونَ

إِلَّآ أَنتُمْ إِنْ شَيْءٍ مِن ٱلرَّحْمَٰنُ أَنزَلَ وَمَآ مِّثْلُنَا بَشَرٌ إِلَّا أَنتُمْ مَآ قَالُوا۟

١٥. تَكْذِبُونَ

١٦. لَمُرْسَلُونَ إِلَيْكُمْ إِنَّآ يَعْلَمُ رَبُّنَا قَالُوا۟

١٧. ٱلْمُبِينُ ٱلْبَلَٰغُ إِلَّا عَلَيْنَآ وَمَا

أَلِيمٌ عَذَابٌ مِّنَّا وَلَيَمَسَّنَّكُم لَنَرْجُمَنَّكُم تَنتَهُوا۟ لَّم لَئِن بِكُم تَطَيَّرْنَا إِنَّا قَالُوا۟

١٨.

١٩. مُّسْرِفُونَ قَوْمٌ أَنتُم بَلْ ذُكِّرْتُم أَئِن مَّعَكُمْ طَٰٓئِرُكُم قَالُوا۟

٢٠. ٱلْمُرْسَلِينَ ٱتَّبِعُوا۟ يَٰقَوْمِ قَالَ يَسْعَىٰ رَجُلٌ ٱلْمَدِينَةِ أَقْصَا مِنْ وَجَآءَ

٢١. مُّهْتَدُونَ وَهُمْ أَجْرًا يَسْـَٔلُكُمْ لَا مَن ٱتَّبِعُوا۟

٢٢. تُرْجَعُونَ وَإِلَيْهِ فَطَرَنِى ٱلَّذِى أَعْبُدُ لَا لِى وَمَا

شَفَٰعَتُهُمْ عَنِّى تُغْنِ لَّا بِضُرٍّ ٱلرَّحْمَٰنُ يُرِدْنِ إِن ءَالِهَةً دُونِهِۦٓ مِن ءَأَتَّخِذُ

٢٣. يُنقِذُونِ وَلَا شَيْـًٔا

٢٤. مُّبِينٍ ضَلَٰلٍ لَّفِى إِذًا إِنِّى

٢٥. فَٱسْمَعُونِ بِرَبِّكُمْ ءَامَنتُ إِنِّى

٢٦. يَعْلَمُونَ قَوْمِى يَٰلَيْتَ قَالَ ٱلْجَنَّةَ ٱدْخُلِ قِيلَ

٢٦. ٱلْمُكْرَمِينَ مِنَ وَجَعَلَنِى رَبِّى غَفَرَ لِى بِمَا

مُنزِلِينَ كُنَّا وَمَا ٱلسَّمَاءِ مِّنَ جُندٍ مِن بَعْدِهِۦ مِنْ قَوْمِهِۦ عَلَىٰ أَنزَلْنَا وَمَآ ٢٨.

٢٩. خَـٰمِدُونَ هُمْ فَإِذَا وَٰحِدَةً صَيْحَةً إِلَّا كَانَتْ إِن

٣٠. يَسْتَهْزِءُونَ بِهِۦ كَانُوا۟ إِلَّا رَسُولٍ مِّن يَأْتِيهِم مَا ٱلْعِبَادِ عَلَى يَـٰحَسْرَةً

٣١. يَرْجِعُونَ لَا إِلَيْهِمْ أَنَّهُمْ ٱلْقُرُونِ مِّنَ قَبْلَهُم أَهْلَكْنَا كَمْ يَرَوْا۟ أَلَمْ

٣٢. مُحْضَرُونَ لَّدَيْنَا جَمِيعٌ لَّمَّا كُلٌّ وَإِن

٣٣. يَأْكُلُونَ فَمِنْهُ مِنْهَا حَبًّا وَأَخْرَجْنَا أَحْيَيْنَـٰهَا ٱلْمَيْتَةُ ٱلْأَرْضُ لَّهُمُ وَءَايَةٌ

٣٤. ٱلْعُيُونِ مِنْ فِيهَا وَفَجَّرْنَا وَأَعْنَـٰبٍ نَّخِيلٍ مِّن جَنَّـٰتٍ فِيهَا وَجَعَلْنَا

٣٥. يَشْكُرُونَ أَفَلَا أَيْدِيهِمْ عَمِلَتْهُ وَمَا ثَمَرِهِۦ مِن لِيَأْكُلُوا۟

٣٦. يَعْلَمُونَ لَا وَمِمَّا أَنفُسِهِمْ وَمِنَ ٱلْأَرْضُ تُنۢبِتُ مِمَّا كُلَّهَا ٱلْأَزْوَٰجَ خَلَقَ ٱلَّذِى سُبْحَـٰنَ

٣٧. مُظْلِمُونَ هُم فَإِذَا ٱلنَّهَارَ مِنْهُ نَسْلَخُ ٱلَّيْلُ لَّهُمُ وَءَايَةٌ

٣٨. ٱلْعَلِيمِ ٱلْعَزِيزِ تَقْدِيرُ ذَٰلِكَ لَهَا لِمُسْتَقَرٍّ تَجْرِى وَٱلشَّمْسُ

٣٩. ٱلْقَدِيمِ كَٱلْعُرْجُونِ عَادَ حَتَّىٰ مَنَازِلَ قَدَّرْنَـٰهُ وَٱلْقَمَرَ

٤٠. فَلَكٍ فِى وَكُلٌّ ٱلنَّهَارِ سَابِقُ ٱلَّيْلُ وَلَا ٱلْقَمَرَ تُدْرِكَ أَن لَهَآ يَنۢبَغِى ٱلشَّمْسُ لَا يَسْبَحُونَ

٤١. ٱلْمَشْحُونِ ٱلْفُلْكِ فِى ذُرِّيَّتَهُمْ حَمَلْنَا أَنَّا لَهُمْ وَءَايَةٌ

٤٢. يَرْكَبُونَ مَا مِّثْلِهِۦ مِّن لَهُم وَخَلَقْنَا

٤٣. يُنقَذُونَ هُمْ وَلَا لَهُمْ صَرِيخَ فَلَا نُغْرِقْهُمْ نَشَأْ وَإِن

٤٤. حِينٍ إِلَىٰ وَمَتَـٰعًا مِّنَّا رَحْمَةً إِلَّا

٤٥. تُرْحَمُونَ لَعَلَّكُمْ خَلْفَكُمْ وَمَا أَيْدِيكُمْ بَيْنَ مَا ٱتَّقُوا۟ ءَاتِيهِمْ قِيلَ وَإِذَا

٤٦. مُعْرِضِينَ عَنْهَا كَانُوا۟ إِلَّا رَبِّهِمْ ءَايَـٰتِ مِّنْ ءَايَةٍ مِّنْ تَأْتِيهِم وَمَا

٤٧. ءَامَنُوا۟ لِلَّذِينَ كَفَرُوا۟ ٱلَّذِينَ قَالَ ٱللَّهُ رَزَقَكُمُ مِمَّا أَنفِقُوا۟ لَهُمْ قِيلَ وَإِذَا

٤٨. مُّبِينٍ ضَلَـٰلٍ فِى إِلَّا أَنتُمْ إِنْ أَطْعَمَهُ ٱللَّهُ يَشَآءُ لَّوْ مَن أَنُطْعِمُ

صَـٰدِقِينَ كُنتُمْ إِن ٱلْوَعْدُ هَـٰذَا مَتَىٰ وَيَقُولُونَ

٤٩. يَخِصِّمُونَ وَهُمْ تَأْخُذُهُمْ وَٰحِدَةً صَيْحَةً إِلَّا يَنظُرُونَ مَا

٥٠. يَرْجِعُونَ أَهْلِهِمْ إِلَىٰ وَلَا تَوْصِيَةً يَسْتَطِيعُونَ فَلَا

٥١. يَنسِلُونَ رَبِّهِمْ إِلَىٰ ٱلْأَجْدَاثِ مِّنَ هُم فَإِذَا ٱلصُّورِ فِى وَنُفِخَ

وَصَدَقَ ٱلرَّحْمَـٰنُ وَعَدَ مَا هَـٰذَا مَّرْقَدِنَا مِنۢ بَعَثَنَا مَن يَـٰوَيْلَنَا قَالُوا۟

٥٢. ٱلْمُرْسَلُونَ

٥٣. مُحْضَرُونَ لَدَيْنَا جَمِيعٌ هُمْ فَإِذَا وَٰحِدَةً صَيْحَةً إِلَّا كَانَتْ إِن

٥٤. تَعْمَلُونَ كُنتُمْ مَا إِلَّا تُجْزَوْنَ وَلَا شَيْـًٔا نَفْسٌ تُظْلَمُ لَا فَٱلْيَوْمَ

٥٥. فَـٰكِهُونَ شُغُلٍ فِى ٱلْيَوْمَ ٱلْجَنَّةِ أَصْحَـٰبَ إِنَّ

٥٦. مُتَّكِـُٔونَ ٱلْأَرَآئِكِ عَلَى ظِلَـٰلٍ فِى وَأَزْوَٰجُهُمْ هُمْ

٥٧. رَحِيمٍ رَّبٍّ مِّن قَوْلًا سَلَـٰمٌ يَدَّعُونَ مَا وَلَهُم فَـٰكِهَةٌ فِيهَا لَهُمْ

٥٩. ٱلْمُجْرِمُونَ أَيُّهَا ٱلْيَوْمَ وَٱمْتَـٰزُوا۟

٦٠. مُّبِينٌ عَدُوٌّ لَكُمْ إِنَّهُ ٱلشَّيْطَـٰنَ تَعْبُدُوا۟ لَا أَن ءَادَمَ يَـٰبَنِىٓ إِلَيْكُمْ أَعْهَدْ أَلَمْ

٦١. مُّسْتَقِيمٌ صِرَٰطٌ هَٰذَا ٱعْبُدُونِى وَأَنِ

٦٢. تَعْقِلُونَ تَكُونُوا۟ أَفَلَمْ ۖ كَثِيرًا جِبِلًّا مِنكُمْ أَضَلَّ وَلَقَدْ

٦٣. تُوعَدُونَ كُنتُمْ ٱلَّتِى جَهَنَّمُ هَٰذِهِۦ

٦٤. تَكْفُرُونَ كُنتُمْ بِمَا ٱلْيَوْمَ ٱصْلَوْهَا

كَانُوا۟ بِمَا أَرْجُلُهُم وَتَشْهَدُ أَيْدِيهِمْ وَتُكَلِّمُنَآ أَفْوَٰهِهِمْ عَلَىٰٓ نَخْتِمُ ٱلْيَوْمَ

٦٥. يَكْسِبُونَ

يُبْصِرُونَ فَأَنَّىٰ ٱلصِّرَٰطَ فَٱسْتَبَقُوا۟ أَعْيُنِهِمْ عَلَىٰٓ لَطَمَسْنَا نَشَآءُ وَلَوْ

يَرْجِعُونَ وَلَا مُضِيًّا ٱسْتَطَٰعُوا۟ فَمَا مَكَانَتِهِمْ عَلَىٰ لَمَسَخْنَٰهُمْ نَشَآءُ وَلَوْ ٦٧

٦٦.

٦٨. يَعْقِلُونَ أَفَلَا ٱلْخَلْقِ فِى نُنَكِّسْهُ نُعَمِّرْهُ وَمَن

٦٩. مُّبِينٌ وَقُرْءَانٌ ذِكْرٌ إِلَّا هُوَ إِنْ لَهُۥٓ يَنۢبَغِى وَمَا ٱلشِّعْرَ عَلَّمْنَٰهُ وَمَا

٧٠. ٱلْكَٰفِرِينَ عَلَى ٱلْقَوْلُ وَيَحِقَّ حَيًّا كَانَ مَن لِّيُنذِرَ

٧١. مَٰلِكُونَ لَهَا فَهُمْ أَنْعَٰمًا أَيْدِينَآ عَمِلَتْ مِّمَّا لَهُمْ خَلَقْنَا أَنَّا يَرَوْا۟ أَوَلَمْ

٧٢. يَأْكُلُونَ وَمِنْهَا رَكُوبُهُمْ فَمِنْهَا لَهُمْ وَذَلَّلْنَٰهَا

٧٣. يَشْكُرُونَ أَفَلَا وَمَشَارِبُ مَنَٰفِعُ فِيهَا وَلَهُمْ

٧٤. يُنصَرُونَ لَعَلَّهُمْ ءَالِهَةً ٱللَّهِ دُونِ مِن وَٱتَّخَذُوا۟

٧٥. مُّحْضَرُونَ جُندٌ لَهُمْ وَهُمْ نَصْرَهُمْ يَسْتَطِيعُونَ لَا

٧٦. يُعْلِنُونَ وَمَا يُسِرُّونَ مَا نَعْلَمُ إِنَّا ۗ قَوْلُهُمْ يَحْزُنكَ فَلَا

٧٧. مُّبِينٌ خَصِيمٌ هُوَ فَإِذَا نُطْفَةٍ مِن خَلَقْنَٰهُ أَنَّا ٱلْإِنسَٰنُ يَرَ أَوَلَمْ

٧٨. رَمِيمٌ وَهِيَ ٱلْعِظَٰمَ يُحْيِ مَن قَالَ خَلْقَهُۥ وَنَسِىَ مَثَلًا لَنَا وَضَرَبَ

٧٩. عَلِيمٌ خَلْقٍ بِكُلِّ وَهُوَ مَرَّةٍ أَوَّلَ أَنشَأَهَآ ٱلَّذِىٓ يُحْيِيهَا قُلْ

٨٠. تُوقِدُونَ مِّنْهُ أَنتُم فَإِذَآ نَارًا ٱلْأَخْضَرِ ٱلشَّجَرِ مِّنَ لَكُم جَعَلَ ٱلَّذِى

٨١. بَلَىٰ مِثْلَهُم يَخْلُقَ أَن عَلَىٰ بِقَٰدِرٍ وَٱلْأَرْضَ ٱلسَّمَٰوَٰتِ خَلَقَ ٱلَّذِى أَوَلَيْسَ ٱلْعَلِيمُ ٱلْخَلَّٰقُ وَهُوَ

٨٢. فَيَكُونُ كُن لَهُۥ يَقُولَ أَن شَيْـًٔا أَرَادَ إِذَآ أَمْرُهُۥٓ إِنَّمَآ

٨٣. تُرْجَعُونَ وَإِلَيْهِ شَىْءٍ كُلِّ مَلَكُوتُ بِيَدِهِۦ ٱلَّذِى فَسُبْحَٰنَ

𝒴our notes:–

"The Heart of the Quran"

Surah Yaseen يٓسٓ

ٱلرَّحِيمِ ٱلرَّحْمَٰنِ ٱللَّهِ بِسْمِ

Bismillah hir rahman nir Raheem

In the name of Allah, the Entirely Merciful, the Especially Merciful

١. يٓسٓ

1. Yaa-Seeen

Yâ-Sîn.

Only Allah knows the meaning

٢. ٱلْحَكِيمِ وَٱلْقُرْءَانِ

Wal-Qur-aanil-Hakeem

By the Glorious Quran, rich in wisdom!

٣. ٱلْمُرْسَلِينَ لَمِنَ إِنَّكَ

3. Innaka laminal mursaleen

You ˹O Prophet˺ are truly one of the messengers

٤. مُسْتَقِيمٍ صِرَطٍ عَلَىٰ

4. 'Alaa Siraatim Mustaqeem

Upon the Straight Path.

٥. ٱلرَّحِيمِ ٱلْعَزِيزِ تَنزِيلَ

5. Tanzeelal 'Azeezir Raheem

ʿThis isʾ a revelation from the Almighty, Most Merciful,

٦. غَـٰفِلُونَ فَهُمْ ءَابَآؤُهُمْ أُنذِرَ مَآ قَوْمًا لِتُنذِرَ

6. Litunzira qawmam maaa unzira aabaaa'uhum fahum ghaafiloon

So that you may warn a people whose forefathers were not warned, and so are heedless.

٧. يُؤْمِنُونَ لَا فَهُمْ أَكْثَرِهِمْ عَلَى ٱلْقَوْلُ حَقَّ لَقَدْ

7. Laqad haqqal qawlu 'alaaa aksarihim fahum laa yu'minoon

The decree ʿof tormentʾ has already been justified against most of them, for they will never believe.

٨. مُّقْمَحُونَ فَهُم ٱلْأَذْقَانِ إِلَى فَهِىَ أَغْلَلًا أَعْنَٰقِهِمْ فِى جَعَلْنَا إِنَّا

8. Innaa ja'alnaa feee a'naaqihim aghlaalan fahiya ilal azqaani fahum muqmahoon

'It is as if' we have put shackles around their necks up to their chins, so their heads are forced up

لَا فَهُمْ فَأَغْشَيْنَٰهُمْ سَدًّا خَلْفِهِم وَمِنْ سَدًّا أَيْدِيهِم بَيْنِ مِنْ وَجَعَلْنَا ٩. يُبْصِرُونَ

9. Wa ja'alnaa mim baini aydeehim saddanw-wa min khalfihim saddan fa aghshai naahum fahum laa yubsiroon

And have placed a barrier before them and a barrier behind them and covered them 'all' up, so they fail to see 'the truth'.

١٠. يُؤْمِنُونَ لَا تُنذِرْهُمْ لَمْ أَمْ ءَأَنذَرْتَهُمْ عَلَيْهِمْ وَسَوَآءٌ

10. Wa sawaaa'un 'alaihim 'a-anzartahum am lam tunzirhum laa yu'minoon

It is the same whether you warn them or not—they will never believe.

وَأَجْرٍ بِمَغْفِرَةٍ فَبَشِّرْهُ بِٱلْغَيْبِ ٱلرَّحْمَـٰنَ وَخَشِيَ ٱلذِّكْرَ ٱتَّبَعَ مَنِ تُنذِرُ إِنَّمَا ١١. كَرِيمٍ

11. Innamaa tunziru manit taba 'az-Zikra wa khashiyar Rahmaana bilghaib, fabashshirhu bimaghfiratinw-wa ajrin kareem

You can only warn those who follow the Reminder1 and are in awe of the Most Compassionate without seeing Him. 2 So give them good news of forgiveness and an honourable reward.

أَحْصَيْنَـٰهُ شَىْءٍ وَكُلَّ وَءَاثَـٰرَهُمْ قَدَّمُوا۟ مَا وَنَكْتُبُ ٱلْمَوْتَىٰ نُحْىِ نَحْنُ إِنَّا ١٢. مُّبِينٍ إِمَامٍ فِىٓ

12. Innaa Nahnu nuhyil mawtaa wa naktubu maa qaddamoo wa aasaarahum; wa kulla shai'in ahsainaahu feee Imaamim Mubeen

It is certainly we who resurrect the dead, and write what they send forth and what they leave behind. Everything is listed by us in a perfect Record.

١٣. ٱلْمُرْسَلُونَ جَآءَهَا إِذِ ٱلْقَرْيَةِ أَصْحَـٰبَ مَّثَلًا لَّهُم وَٱضْرِب

13. Wadrib lahum masalan Ashaabal Qaryatih; iz jaaa'ahal mursaloon

Give them an example ˹O Prophet˺ of the residents of a town, when the messengers came to them.

إِلَيْكُم إِنَّا فَقَالُوا بِثَالِثٍ فَعَزَّزْنَا فَكَذَّبُوهُمَا ٱثْنَيْنِ إِلَيْهِم أَرْسَلْنَآ إِذْ
١٤. مُرْسَلُونَ

14. Iz arsalnaaa ilaihimusnaini fakazzaboohumaa fa'azzaznaa bisaalisin faqaalooo innaaa ilaikum mursaloon

We sent them two messengers, but they rejected both. So, we reinforced ˹the two˺ with a third, and they declared, "We have indeed been sent to you ˹as messengers˺."

إِلَّا أَنتُم إِنْ شَيْءٍ مِن ٱلرَّحْمَـٰنُ أَنزَلَ وَمَآ مِّثْلُنَا بَشَرٌ إِلَّا أَنتُم مَّآ قَالُوا
١٥. تَكْذِبُونَ

15. Qaaloo maaa antum illaa basharum mislunaa wa maaa anzalar Rahmaanu min shai'in in antum illaa takziboon

The people replied, "You are only humans like us, and the Most Compassionate has not revealed anything. You are simply lying!"

١٦. لَمُرْسَلُونَ إِلَيْكُم إِنَّآ يَعْلَمُ رَبُّنَا قَالُوا

16. Qaaloo Rabbunaa ya'lamu innaaa ilaikum lamursaloon

The messengers responded, "Our Lord knows that we have truly been sent to you.

١٧. ٱلْمُبِينُ ٱلْبَلَـٰغُ إِلَّا عَلَيْنَآ وَمَا

17. Wa maa 'alainaaa illal balaaghul mubeen

And our duty is only to deliver ˹the message˺ clearly."

أَلِيمٌ عَذَابٌ مِّنَّا وَلَيَمَسَّنَّكُمْ لَنَرْجُمَنَّكُمْ تَنتَهُوا۟ لَّمْ لَئِنۛبِكُمْ تَطَيَّرْنَا إِنَّا قَالُوٓا۟ ١٨.

18. Qaaloo innaa tataiyarnaa bikum la'il-lam tantahoo lanar jumannakum wa la-yamassan nakum minnaa 'azaabun aleem

The people replied, "We definitely see you as a bad omen for us. If you do not desist, we will certainly stone you ˹to death˺ and you will be touched with a painful punishment from us."

١٩. مُّسْرِفُونَ قَوْمٌ أَنتُم بَلْۛ ذُكِّرْتُمْ أَئِنۛ مَّعَكُمْ طَٰٓئِرُكُم قَالُوٓا۟

19. Qaaloo taaa'irukum ma'akum; a'in zukkirtum; bal antum qawmum musrifoon

The messengers said, "Your bad omen lies within yourselves. Are you saying this because you are reminded ˹of the truth˺? In fact, you are a transgressing people."

٢٠. ٱلْمُرْسَلِينَ ٱتَّبِعُوا۟ يَٰقَوْمِ قَالَ يَسْعَىٰ رَجُلٌ ٱلْمَدِينَةِ أَقْصَا مِنْ وَجَآءَ

20. Wa jaaa'a min aqsal madeenati rajuluny yas'aa qaala yaa qawmit tabi'ul mursaleen

Then from the farthest end of the city a man came, rushing. He advised, "O my people! Follow the messengers.

٢١. مُهْتَدُونَ وَهُم أَجْرًا يَسْـَٔلُكُمْ لَّا مَنْ ٱتَّبِعُوٓا۟

21. Ittabi'oo mal-laa yas'alukum ajranw-wa hum muhtadoon

Follow those who ask no reward of you, and are ˹rightly˺ guided.

٢٢. تُرْجَعُونَ وَإِلَيْهِ فَطَرَنِى ٱلَّذِى أَعْبُدُ لَآ لِىَ وَمَا

22. Wa maa liya laaa a'budul lazee fataranee wa ilaihi turja'oon

And why should I not worship the One who has originated me, and to whom you will be returned.

شَفَٰعَتُهُمْ عَنِّى تُغْنِ لَّا بِضُرٍّ ٱلرَّحْمَٰنُ يُرِدْنِ إِن ءَالِهَةً دُونِهِۦٓ مِن ءَأَتَّخِذُ
٢٣. يُنقِذُونِ وَلَا شَيْـًٔا

23. 'A-attakhizu min dooniheee aalihatan iny-yuridnir Rahmaanu bidurril-laa tughni 'annee shafaa 'atuhum shai 'anw-wa laa yunqizoon

How could I take besides Him other gods whose intercession would not be of any benefit to me, nor could they save me if the Most Compassionate intended to harm me?

٢٤. مُّبِينٍ ضَلَٰلٍ لَّفِى إِذًا إِنَّ

24. Inneee izal-lafee dalaa-lim-mubeen

Indeed, I would then be clearly astray.

٢٥. فَٱسْمَعُونِ بِرَبِّكُمْ ءَامَنتُ إِنِّ

25. Inneee aamantu bi Rabbikum fasma'oon

I do believe in your Lord, so listen to me."

٢٦. يَعْلَمُونَ قَوْمِى يَٰلَيْتَ قَالَ ٱلْجَنَّةَ ٱدْخُلِ قِيلَ

26. Qeelad khulil Jannnah; qaala yaa laita qawmee ya'lamoon

ʿBut they killed him, thenʾ he was told ʿby the angelsʾ, "Enter Paradise!" He said, "If only my people knew

٢٦. ٱلْمُكْرَمِينَ مِنَ وَجَعَلَنِى رَبِّى لِى غَفَرَ بِمَا

27. Bimaa ghafara lee Rabbee wa ja'alanee minal mukrameen

Of how my Lord has forgiven me, and made me one of the honorable."

مُنزِلِينَ كُنَّا وَمَا ٱلسَّمَآءِ مِّنَ جُندٍ مِن بَعْدِهِۦ مِن قَوْمِهِۦ عَلَىٰ أَنزَلْنَا وَمَآ
٢٨.

28. Wa maaa anzalnaa 'alaa qawmihee mim ba'dihee min jundim minas-samaaa'i wa maa kunnaa munzileen

We did not send any soldiers from the heavens against his people after his death, nor did we need to.

٢٩. خَـٰمِدُونَ هُمْ فَإِذَا وَحِدَةً صَيْحَةً إِلَّا كَانَتْ إِن

29. In kaanat illaa saihatanw waahidatan fa-izaa hum khaamidoon

All it took was one 'mighty' blast, and they were extinguished at once.

٣٠. يَسْتَهْزِءُونَ بِهِۦ كَانُوٓاْ إِلَّا رَّسُولٍ مِّن يَأْتِيهِم مَّا ٱلْعِبَادِ عَلَى يَـٰحَسْرَةً

30. Yaa hasratan 'alal 'ibaad; maa yaateehim mir Rasoolin illaa kaanoo bihee yastahzi 'oon

Oh pity, such beings! No messenger ever came to them without being mocked.

٣١. يَرْجِعُونَ لَا إِلَيْهِمْ أَنَّهُمْ ٱلْقُرُونِ مِّن قَبْلَهُم أَهْلَكْنَا كَمْ يَرَوْاْ أَلَمْ

31. Alam yaraw kam ahlak naa qablahum minal qurooni annahum ilaihim laa yarji'oon

Have the deniers not considered how many peoples we destroyed before them who never came back to life again?

٣٢. مُحْضَرُونَ لَدَيْنَا جَمِيعٌ لَّمَّا كُلٌّ وَإِن

32. Wa in kullul lammaa jamee'ul-ladainaa muhdaroon

Yet they will all be brought before us.

٣٣. يَأْكُلُونَ فَمِنْهُ حَبًّا مِنْهَا وَأَخْرَجْنَا أَحْيَيْنَـٰهَا ٱلْمَيْتَةُ ٱلْأَرْضُ لَهُمْ وَءَايَةٌ

33. Wa Aayatul lahumul ardul maitatu ahyainaahaa wa akhrajnaa minhaa habban faminhu yaakuloon

There is a sign for them in the dead earth: We give it life, producing grain from it for them to eat.

٣٤. ٱلْعُيُونِ مِنَ فِيهَا وَفَجَّرْنَا وَأَعْنَـٰبٍ نَّخِيلٍ مِّن جَنَّـٰتٍ فِيهَا وَجَعَلْنَا

34. Wa ja'alnaa feehaa jannaatim min nakheelinw wa a'naabinw wa fajjarnaa feeha minal 'uyoon

And we have placed in it gardens of palm trees and grapevines, and caused springs to gush forth in it,

٣٥. يَشْكُرُونَ أَفَلَا أَيْدِيهِمْ عَمِلَتْهُ وَمَا ثَمَرِهِۦ مِن لِيَأْكُلُوا۟

35. Liyaakuloo min samarihee wa maa 'amilat-hu aideehim; afalaa yashkuroon

So that they may eat from its fruit, which they had no hand in making. Will they not then give thanks?

٣٦. لَا وَمِمَّا أَنفُسِهِمْ وَمِنَ ٱلْأَرْضُ تُنۢبِتُ مِمَّا كُلَّهَا ٱلْأَزْوَٰجَ خَلَقَ ٱلَّذِى سُبْحَـٰنَ يَعْلَمُونَ

36. Subhaanal lazee khalaqal azwaaja kullahaa mimmaa tumbitul ardu wa min anfusihim wa mimmaa laa ya'lamoon

Glory be to the One Who created all ˹things in˺ pairs—˹be it˺ what the earth produces, their genders, or what they do not know!

٣٧. مُظْلِمُونَ هُم فَإِذَا ٱلنَّهَارَ مِنْهُ نَسْلَخُ ٱلَّيْلُ لَّهُمْ وَءَايَةٌ

37. Wa Aayatul lahumul lailu naslakhu minhun nahaara fa-izaa hum muzlimoon

There is also a sign for them in the night: We strip from it daylight, then—behold! —they are in darkness.

٣٨. ٱلْعَلِيمِ ٱلْعَزِيزِ تَقْدِيرُ ذَٰلِكَ لَّهَا لِمُسْتَقَرٍّ تَجْرِى وَٱلشَّمْسُ

38. Wash-shamsu tajree limustaqarril lahaa; zaalika taqdeerul 'Azeezil Aleem

The sun travels for its fixed term. That is the design of the Almighty, All-Knowing.

٣٩. ٱلْقَدِيمِ كَٱلْعُرْجُونِ عَادَ حَتَّىٰ مَنَازِلَ قَدَّرْنَٰهُ وَٱلْقَمَرَ

39. Walqamara qaddarnaahu manaazila hattaa 'aada kal'ur joonil qadeem

As for the moon, we have ordained ˈpreciseˈ phases for it, until it ends up like an old, curved palm stalk.

فَلَكٍ فِى وَكُلٌّ ٱلنَّهَارِ سَابِقُ ٱلَّيْلُ وَلَا ٱلْقَمَرَ تُدْرِكَ أَن لَهَآ يَنْبَغِى ٱلشَّمْسُ لَا
٤٠. يَسْبَحُونَ

40. Lash shamsu yambaghee lahaaa an tudrikal qamara wa lal lailu saabiqun nahaar; wa kullun fee falaki yasbahoon

It is not for the sun to catch up with the moon, 1 nor does the night outrun the day. Each is travelling in an orbit of their own.

٤١. ٱلْمَشْحُونِ ٱلْفُلْكِ فِى ذُرِّيَّتَهُمْ حَمَلْنَا أَنَّا لَهُمْ وَءَايَةٌ

41. Wa Aayatul lahum annaa hamalnaa zurriyatahum fil fulkil mashhoon

Another sign for them is that we carried their ancestor's ˹with Noah˺ in the fully loaded Ark,

٤٢. يَرْكَبُونَ مَا مِّثْلِهِۦ مِّن لَهُم وَخَلَقْنَا

42. Wa khalaqnaa lahum mim-mislihee maa yarkaboon

And created for them similar things to ride in.

٤٣. يُنقَذُونَ هُمْ وَلَا لَهُمْ صَرِيخَ فَلَا نُغْرِقْهُمْ نَّشَأْ وَإِن

43. Wa in nashaa nughriqhum falaa sareekha lahum wa laa hum yunqazoon

If we willed, we could drown them: then no one would respond to their cries, nor would they be rescued—

٤٤. حِينٍ إِلَىٰ وَمَتَـٰعًا مِّنَّا رَحْمَةً إِلَّا

44. Illaa rahmatam minnaa wa mataa'an ilaa heen

Except by mercy from us, allowing them enjoyment for a ˹little˺ while.

٤٥. تُرْحَمُونَ لَعَلَّكُمْ خَلْفَكُمْ وَمَا أَيْدِيكُم بَيْنَ مَا ٱتَّقُوا لَهُم قِيلَ وَإِذَا

45. Wa izaa qeela lahumuttaqoo maa baina aideekum wa maa khalfakum la'allakum turhamoon

'Still they turn away' when it is said to them, "Beware of what is ahead of you 'in the Hereafter' and what is behind you 'of destroyed nations' so you may be shown mercy."

٤٦. مُعْرِضِينَ عَنْهَا كَانُوا إِلَّا رَبِّهِمْ ءَايَٰتِ مِّنْ ءَايَةٍ مِّنْ تَأْتِيهِم وَمَا

46. Wa maa taateehim min aayatim min ayataati Rabbihim illaa kaanoo 'anhaa mu'rideen

Whenever a sign comes to them from their Lord, they turn away from it.

ءَامَنُوا لِلَّذِينَ كَفَرُوا ٱلَّذِينَ قَالَ ٱللَّهُ رَزَقَكُمُ مِمَّا أَنفِقُوا لَهُمْ قِيلَ وَإِذَا
٤٧. مُّبِينٍ ضَلَٰلٍ فِى إِلَّا أَنتُمْ إِنْ أَطْعَمَهُ ٱللَّهُ يَشَاءُ لَّوْ مَن أَنُطْعِمُ

47. Wa izaa qeela lahum anfiqoo mimmaa razaqakumul laahu qaalal lazeena kafaroo lillazeena aamanooo anut'imu mal-law yashaaa'ul laahu at'amahooo in antum illaa fee dalaalim Mubeen

And when it is said to them, "Donate from what Allah has provided for you," the disbelievers say to the believers, "Why should we feed those whom Allah could have fed if He wanted to? You are clearly astray!"

٤٨. صَـٰدِقِينَ كُنتُمْ إِن ٱلْوَعْدُ هَـٰذَا مَتَىٰ وَيَقُولُونَ

48. Wa yaqooloona mataa haazal wa'du in kuntum saadiqeen

And they ask ˹the believers˺, "When will this threat come to pass, if what you say is true?"

٤٩. يَخِصِّمُونَ وَهُمْ تَأْخُذُهُمْ وَٰحِدَةً صَيْحَةً إِلَّا يَنظُرُونَ مَا

49. Maa yanzuroona illaa saihatanw waahidatan taa khuzuhum wa hum yakhissimoon

They must be awaiting a single Blast, 1 which will seize them while they are ˹entrenched˺ in ˹worldly˺ disputes.

٥٠. يَرْجِعُونَ أَهْلِهِمْ إِلَىٰ وَلَا تَوْصِيَةً يَسْتَطِيعُونَ فَلَا

50. Falaa yastatee'oona taw siyatanw-wa laaa ilaaa ahlihim yarji'oon

Then they will not be able to make a ˹last˺ will, nor can they return to their own people.

٥١. يَنسِلُونَ رَبِّهِمْ إِلَىٰ ٱلْأَجْدَاثِ مِّنَ هُم فَإِذَا ٱلصُّورِ فِى وَنُفِخَ

51. Wa nufikha fis-soori faizaa hum minal ajdaasi ilaa Rabbihim yansiloon

The Trumpet will be blown ˹a second time˺, then—behold! —they will rush from the graves to their Lord.

وَصَدَقَ ٱلرَّحْمَٰنُ وَعَدَ مَا هَٰذَا مَّرْقَدِنَا مِن بَعَثَنَا مَن يَٰوَيْلَنَا قَالُوا۟
٥٢. ٱلْمُرْسَلُونَ

52. Qaaloo yaa wailanaa mam ba'asanaa mim marqadinaa; haaza maa wa'adar Rahmanu wa sadaqal mursaloon

They will cry, "Woe to us! Who has raised us up from our place of rest? This must be what the Most Compassionate warned us of; the messengers told the truth!"

مُحْضَرُونَ لَّدَيْنَا جَمِيعٌ هُمْ فَإِذَا وَٰحِدَةً صَيْحَةً إِلَّا كَانَتْ إِن ٥٣.

53. In kaanat illaa saihatanw waahidatan fa-izaa hum jamee'ul ladainaa muhdaroon

It will only take one Blast, then at once they will all be brought before us.

تَعْمَلُونَ كُنتُمْ مَا إِلَّا تُجْزَوْنَ وَلَا شَيْئًا نَفْسٌ تُظْلَمُ لَا فَٱلْيَوْمَ ٥٤.

54. Fal-Yawma laa tuzlamu nafsun shai'anw-wa laa tujzawna illaa maa kuntum ta'maloon

On that Day no soul will be wronged in the least, nor will you be rewarded except for what you used to do.

فَٰكِهُونَ شُغُلٍ فِي ٱلْيَوْمَ ٱلْجَنَّةِ أَصْحَٰبَ إِنَّ ٥٥.

55. Inna Ashaabal jannatil Yawma fee shughulin faakihoon

Indeed, on that Day the residents of Paradise will be busy enjoying themselves.

٥٦. مُتَّكِئُونَ ٱلْأَرَائِكِ عَلَى ظِلَلٍ فِي وَأَزْوَاجُهُمْ هُمْ

56. Hum wa azwaajuhum fee zilaalin 'alal araaa'iki muttaki'oon

They and their spouses will be in ˹cool˺ shade, reclining on ˹canopied˺ couches.

٥٧. يَدَّعُونَ مَّا وَلَهُم فَٰكِهَةٌ فِيهَا لَهُمْ

57. Lahum feehaa faakiha tunw-wa lahum maa yadda'oon

There they will have fruits and whatever they desire.

٥٨. رَّحِيمٍ رَّبٍّ مِّن قَوْلًا سَلَٰمٌ

58. Salaamun qawlam mir Rabbir Raheem

And "Peace!" will be ˹their˺ greeting from the Merciful Lord.

٥٩. ٱلْمُجْرِمُونَ أَيُّهَا ٱلْيَوْمَ وَٱمْتَٰزُواْ

59. Wamtaazul Yawma ayyuhal mujrimoon

˹Then the disbelievers will be told,˺ "Step away ˹from the believers˺ this Day, O wicked ones!

٦٠. مُبِينٌ عَدُوٌّ لَكُمْ إِنَّهُۥ ٱلشَّيْطَٰنَ تَعْبُدُوا۟ لَّا أَن ءَادَمَ يَٰبَنِىٓ إِلَيْكُمْ أَعْهَدْ أَلَمْ

60. Alam a'had ilaikum yaa Baneee Aadama al-laa ta'budush Shaitaana innahoo lakum 'aduwwum Mubeen

Did I not command you, O Children of Adam, not to follow Satan, for he is truly your sworn enemy?

٦١. مُّسْتَقِيمٌ صِرَٰطٌ هَٰذَا ٱعْبُدُونِى وَأَنِ

61. Wa ani'budoonee; haazaa Siraatum Mustaqeem

But to worship me ˹alone˺? This is the Straight Path.

٦٢. تَعْقِلُونَ تَكُونُوا۟ أَفَلَمْ كَثِيرًا جِبِلًّا مِنكُمْ أَضَلَّ وَلَقَدْ

62. Wa laqad adalla minkum jibillan kaseeraa; afalam takoonoo ta'qiloon

Yet he already misled great multitudes of you. Did you not have any sense?

٦٣. تُوعَدُونَ كُنتُمْ ٱلَّتِى جَهَنَّمُ هَٰذِهِۦ

63. Haazihee Jahannamul latee kuntum too'adoon

This is the Hell you were warned of.

٦٤. تَكْفُرُونَ كُنتُم بِمَا ٱلْيَوْمَ ٱصْلَوْهَا

64. Islawhal Yawma bimaa kuntum takfuroon

Burn in it today for your disbelief."

كَانُواْ بِمَا أَرْجُلُهُم وَتَشْهَدُ أَيْدِيهِم وَتُكَلِّمُنَآ أَفْوَٰهِهِم عَلَىٰ نَخْتِمُ ٱلْيَوْمَ
٦٥. يَكْسِبُونَ

65. Al-Yawma nakhtimu 'alaaa afwaahihim wa tukallimunaaa aideehim
wa tashhadu arjuluhum bimaa kaanoo yaksiboon

On this Day We will seal their mouths, their hands will speak to us,
and their feet will testify to what they used to commit.

٦٦. يُبْصِرُونَ فَأَنَّى ٱلصِّرَٰطَ فَٱسْتَبَقُواْ أَعْيُنِهِم عَلَىٰ لَطَمَسْنَا نَشَآءُ وَلَوْ

66. Wa law nashaaa'u lata masna 'alaaa aiyunihim fasta baqus-siraata
fa-annaa yubsiroon

Had we willed, we could have easily blinded their eyes, so they would
struggle to find their way. How then could they see?

٦٧. يَرْجِعُونَ وَلَا مُضِيًّا ٱسْتَطَٰعُواْ فَمَا مَكَانَتِهِم عَلَىٰ لَمَسَخْنَٰهُم نَشَآءُ وَلَوْ

67. Wa law nashaaa'u lamasakhnaahum 'alaa makaanatihim famastataa'oo mudiyyanw-wa laa yarji'oon

And had we willed, we could have transfigured them on the spot, 1 so
they could neither progress forward nor turn back.

٦٨. يَعْقِلُونَ أَفَلَا ٱلْخَلْقِ فِى نُنَكِّسْهُ نُعَمِّرْهُ وَمَن

68. Wa man nu 'ammirhu nunakkishu fil-khalq; afalaa ya'qiloon

And whoever we grant a long life, we reverse them in development.1
Will they not then understand?

٦٩. مُّبِينٌ وَقُرْءَانٌ ذِكْرٌ إِلَّا هُوَ إِنْ لَهُۥ يَنْبَغِى وَمَا ٱلشِّعْرَ عَلَّمْنَهُ وَمَا

69. Wa maa 'allamnaahush shi'ra wa maa yambaghee lah; in huwa illaa
zikrunw-wa Qur-aanum Mubeen

We have not taught him poetry, nor is it fitting for him. This ˹Book˺ is
only a Reminder and a clear Quran.

٧٠. ٱلْكَٰفِرِينَ عَلَى ٱلْقَوْلُ وَيَحِقَّ حَيًّا كَانَ مَن لِّيُنذِرَ

70. Liyunzira man kaana haiyanw-wa yahiqqal qawlu 'alal-kaafireen

To warn whoever is ˹truly˺ alive and fulfil the decree ˹of torment˺
against the disbelievers.

٧١. مَٰلِكُونَ لَهَا فَهُمْ أَنْعَٰمًا أَيْدِينَا عَمِلَتْ مِّمَّا لَهُم خَلَقْنَا أَنَّا يَرَوْا أَوَلَمْ

71. Awalam yaraw annaa khalaqnaa lahum mimmaa 'amilat aideenaaa
an'aaman fahum lahaa maalikoon

Do they not see that we singlehandedly1 created for them, among
other things, cattle which are under their control?

٧٢. يَأْكُلُونَ وَمِنْهَا رَكُوبُهُمْ فَمِنْهَا لَهُمْ وَذَلَّلْنَـٰهَا

72. Wa zallalnaahaa lahum faminhaa rakoobuhum wa minhaa yaakuloon

And we have subjected these ˹animals˺ to them, so they may ride some and eat others.

٧٣. يَشْكُرُونَ أَفَلَا وَمَشَارِبُ مَنَـٰفِعُ فِيهَا وَلَهُمْ

73. Wa lahum feehaa manaa fi'u wa mashaarib; afalaa yashkuroon

And they derive from them other benefits and drinks. Will they not then give thanks?

٧٤. يُنصَرُونَ لَعَلَّهُمْ ءَالِهَةً ٱللَّهِ دُونِ مِن وَٱتَّخَذُوا

74. Wattakhazoo min doonil laahi aalihatal la'allahum yunsaroon

Still, they have taken other gods besides Allah, hoping to be helped ˹by them˺.

٧٥. مُحْضَرُونَ جُندٌ لَهُمْ وَهُمْ نَصْرَهُمْ يَسْتَطِيعُونَ لَا

75. Laa yastatee'oona nasrahum wa hum lahum jundum muhdaroon

They cannot help the pagans, even though they serve the idols as dedicated guards.

٧٦. يُعْلِنُونَ وَمَا يُسِرُّونَ مَا نَعْلَمُ إِنَّا قَوْلُهُمْ يَحْزُنكَ فَلَا

76. Falaa yahzunka qawluhum; innaa na'lamu maa yusirroona wa maa yu'linoon

So do not let their words grieve you ˹O Prophet˺. Indeed, we ˹fully˺ know what they conceal and what they reveal.

٧٧. مُّبِينٌ خَصِيمٌ هُوَ فَإِذَا نُطْفَةٍ مِن خَلَقْنَهُ أَنَّا ٱلْإِنسَـٰنُ يَرَ أَوَلَمْ

77. Awalam yaral insaanu annaa khalaqnaahu min nutfatin fa-izaa huwa khaseemum Mubeen

Do people not see that we have created them from a sperm-drop, then—behold! —they openly challenge ˹Us˺?

٧٨. رَمِيمٌ وَهِيَ ٱلْعِظَـٰمَ يُحْيِ مَن قَالَ خَلْقَهُۥ وَنَسِيَ مَثَلًا لَنَا وَضَرَبَ

78. Wa daraba lanaa maslanw-wa nasiya khalqahoo qaala mai-yuhyil'izaama wa hiya rameem

And they argue with us—forgetting they were created—saying, "Who will give life to decayed bones?"

٧٩. عَلِيمٌ خَلْقٍ بِكُلِّ وَهُوَ مَرَّةٍ أَوَّلَ أَنشَأَهَآ ٱلَّذِىٓ يُحْيِيهَا قُلْ

79. Qul yuh yeehal lazeee ansha ahaaa awwala marrah; wa Huwa bikulli khalqin 'Aleem

Say, ˹O Prophet, ˺ "They will be revived by the One who produced them the first time, for He has ˹perfect˺ knowledge of every created being.

٨٠. تُوقِدُونَ مِّنْهُ أَنتُم فَإِذَآ أَنتُم نَارًا ٱلْأَخْضَرِ ٱلشَّجَرِ مِّنَ لَكُم جَعَلَ ٱلَّذِى

80. Allazee ja'ala lakum minash shajaril akhdari naaran fa-izaaa antum minhu tooqidoon

'He is the One' Who gives you fire from green trees, and—behold!—you kindle 'fire' from them.

بَلَىٰ مِثْلَهُم يَخْلُقَ أَن عَلَىٰ بِقَـٰدِرٍ وَٱلْأَرْضَ ٱلسَّمَـٰوَٰتِ خَلَقَ ٱلَّذِى أَوَلَيْسَ ٨١. ٱلْعَلِيمُ ٱلْخَلَّـٰقُ وَهُوَ

81. Awa laisal lazee khalaqas samaawaati wal arda biqaadirin 'alaaa ai-yakhluqa mislahum; balaa wa Huwal Khallaaqul 'Aleem

Can the One Who created the heavens and the earth not 'easily' resurrect these 'deniers'?" Yes 'He can'! For He is the Master Creator, All-Knowing.

٨٢. فَيَكُونُ كُن لَهُ يَقُولَ أَن شَيْئًا أَرَادَ إِذَآ أَمْرُهُ إِنَّمَآ

82. Innamaa amruhooo izaaa araada shai'an ai-yaqoola lahoo Kun fa-yakoon

All it takes, when He wills something 'to be', is simply to say to it: "Be!" And it is!

٨٣. تُرْجَعُونَ وَإِلَيْهِ شَىْءٍ كُلَّ مَلَكُوتُ بِيَدِهِۦ ٱلَّذِى فَسُبْحَـٰنَ

83. Fa Subhaanal lazee biyadihee malakootu kulli shai-inw-wa ilaihi turja'oon

So, glory be to the One in Whose Hands is the authority over all things, and to whom ˹alone˺ you will ˹all˺ be returned.

Surah Yaseen

يٰسٓ

Pronunciation

1. Yaa-Seeen

2. Wal-Qur-aanil-Hakeem

3. Innaka laminal mursaleen

4. 'Alaa Siraatim Mustaqeem

5. Tanzeelal 'Azeezir Raheem

6. Litunzira qawmam maaa unzira aabaaa'uhum fahum ghaafiloon

7. Laqad haqqal qawlu 'alaaa aksarihim fahum laa yu'minoon

8. Innaa ja'alnaa feee a'naaqihim aghlaalan fahiya ilal azqaani fahum muqmahoon

9. Wa ja'alnaa mim baini aydeehim saddanw-wa min khalfihim saddan fa aghshai naahum fahum laa yubsiroon

10. Wa sawaaa'un 'alaihim 'a-anzartahum am lam tunzirhum laa yu'minoon

11. Innamaa tunziru manit taba 'az-Zikra wa khashiyar Rahmaana bilghaib, fabashshirhu bimaghfiratinw-wa ajrin kareem

12. Innaa Nahnu nuhyil mawtaa wa naktubu maa qaddamoo wa aasaarahum; wa kulla shai'in ahsainaahu feee Imaamim Mubeen

13. Wadrib lahum masalan Ashaabal Qaryatih; iz jaaa'ahal mursaloon

14. Iz arsalnaaa ilaihimusnaini fakazzaboohumaa fa'azzaznaa bisaalisin faqaalooo innaaa ilaikum mursaloon

15. Qaaloo maaa antum illaa basharum mislunaa wa maaa anzalar Rahmaanu min shai'in in antum illaa takziboon

16. Qaaloo Rabbunaa ya'lamu innaaa ilaikum lamursaloon

17. Wa maa 'alainaaa illal balaaghul mubeen

18. Qaaloo innaa tataiyarnaa bikum la'il-lam tantahoo lanar jumannakum wa la-yamassan nakum minnaa 'azaabun aleem

19. Qaaloo taaa'irukum ma'akum; a'in zukkirtum; bal antum qawmum musrifoon

20. Wa jaaa'a min aqsal madeenati rajuluny yas'aa qaala yaa qawmit tabi'ul mursaleen

21. Ittabi'oo mal-laa yas'alukum ajranw-wa hum muhtadoon

22. Wa maa liya laaa a'budul lazee fataranee wa ilaihi turja'oon

23. 'A-attakhizu min dooniheee aalihatan iny-yuridnir Rahmaanu bidurril-laa tughni 'annee shafaa 'atuhum shai 'anw-wa laa yunqizoon

24. Inneee izal-lafee dalaa-lim-mubeen

25. Inneee aamantu bi Rabbikum fasma'oon

26. Qeelad khulil Jannnah; qaala yaa laita qawmee ya'lamoon

27. Bimaa ghafara lee Rabbee wa ja'alanee minal mukrameen

28. Wa maaa anzalnaa 'alaa qawmihee mim ba'dihee min jundim minas-samaaa'i wa maa kunnaa munzileen

29. In kaanat illaa saihatanw waahidatan fa-izaa hum khaamidoon

30. Yaa hasratan 'alal 'ibaad; maa yaateehim mir Rasoolin illaa kaanoo bihee yastahzi 'oon

31. Alam yaraw kam ahlak naa qablahum minal qurooni annahum ilaihim laa yarji'oon

32. Wa in kullul lammaa jamee'ul-ladainaa muhdaroon

33. Wa Aayatul lahumul ardul maitatu ahyainaahaa wa akhrajnaa minhaa habban faminhu yaakuloon

34. Wa ja'alnaa feehaa jannaatim min nakheelinw wa a'naabinw wa fajjarnaa feeha minal 'uyoon

35. Liyaakuloo min samarihee wa maa 'amilat-hu aideehim; afalaa yashkuroon

36. Subhaanal lazee khalaqal azwaaja kullahaa mimmaa tumbitul ardu wa min anfusihim wa mimmaa laa ya'lamoon

37. Wa Aayatul lahumul lailu naslakhu minhun nahaara fa-izaa hum muzlimoon

38. Wash-shamsu tajree limustaqarril lahaa; zaalika taqdeerul 'Azeezil Aleem

39. Walqamara qaddarnaahu manaazila hattaa 'aada kal'ur joonil qadeem

40. Lash shamsu yambaghee lahaaa an tudrikal qamara wa lal lailu saabiqun nahaar; wa kullun fee falaki yasbahoon

41. Wa Aayatul lahum annaa hamalnaa zurriyatahum fil fulkil mashhoon

42. Wa khalaqnaa lahum mim-mislihee maa yarkaboon

43. Wa in nashaa nughriqhum falaa sareekha lahum wa laa hum yunqazoon

44. Illaa rahmatam minnaa wa mataa'an ilaa heen

45. Wa izaa qeela lahumuttaqoo maa baina aideekum wa maa khalfakum la'allakum turhamoon

46. Wa maa taateehim min aayatim min ayataati Rabbihim illaa kaanoo 'anhaa mu'rideen

47. Wa izaa qeela lahum anfiqoo mimmaa razaqakumul laahu qaalal lazeena kafaroo lillazeena aamanooo anut'imu mal-law yashaaa'ul laahu at'amahooo in antum illaa fee dalaalim mubeen

48. Wa yaqooloona mataa haazal wa'du in kuntum saadiqeen

49. Maa yanzuroona illaa saihatanw waahidatan taa khuzuhum wa hum yakhissimoon

50. Falaa yastatee'oona taw siyatanw-wa laaa ilaaa ahlihim yarji'oon

51. Wa nufikha fis-soori faizaa hum minal ajdaasi ilaa Rabbihim yansiloon

52. Qaaloo yaa wailanaa mam ba'asanaa mim marqadinaa; haaza maa wa'adar Rahmanu wa sadaqal mursaloon

53. In kaanat illaa saihatanw waahidatan fa-izaa hum jamee'ul ladainaa muhdaroon

54. Fal-Yawma laa tuzlamu nafsun shai'anw-wa laa tujzawna illaa maa kuntum ta'maloon

55. Inna Ashaabal jannatil Yawma fee shughulin faakihoon

56. Hum wa azwaajuhum fee zilaalin 'alal araaa'iki muttaki'oon

57. Lahum feehaa faakiha tunw-wa lahum maa yadda'oon

58. Salaamun qawlam mir Rabbir Raheem

59. Wamtaazul Yawma ayyuhal mujrimoon

60. Alam a'had ilaikum yaa Baneee Aadama al-laa ta'budush Shaitaana innahoo lakum 'aduwwum mubeen

61. Wa ani'budoonee; haazaa Siraatum Mustaqeem

62. Wa laqad adalla minkum jibillan kaseeraa; afalam takoonoo ta'qiloon

63. Haazihee Jahannamul latee kuntum too'adoon

64. Islawhal Yawma bimaa kuntum takfuroon

65. Al-Yawma nakhtimu 'alaaa afwaahihim wa tukallimunaaa aideehim wa tashhadu arjuluhum bimaa kaanoo yaksiboon

66. Wa law nashaaa'u lata masna 'alaaa aiyunihim fasta baqus-siraata fa-annaa yubsiroon

67. Wa law nashaaa'u lamasakhnaahum 'alaa makaanatihim famastataa'oo mudiyyanw-wa laa yarji'oon

68. Wa man nu 'ammirhu nunakkishu fil-khalq; afalaa ya'qiloon

69. Wa maa 'allamnaahush shi'ra wa maa yambaghee lah; in huwa illaa zikrunw-wa Qur-aanum mubeen

70. Liyunzira man kaana haiyanw-wa yahiqqal qawlu 'alal-kaafireen

71. Awalam yaraw annaa khalaqnaa lahum mimmaa 'amilat aideenaaa an'aaman fahum lahaa maalikoon

72. Wa zallalnaahaa lahum faminhaa rakoobuhum wa minhaa yaakuloon

73. Wa lahum feehaa manaa fi'u wa mashaarib; afalaa yashkuroon

74. Wattakhazoo min doonil laahi aalihatal la'allahum yunsaroon

75. Laa yastatee'oona nasrahum wa hum lahum jundum muhdaroon

76. Falaa yahzunka qawluhum; innaa na'lamu maa yusirroona wa maa yu'linoon

77. Awalam yaral insaanu annaa khalaqnaahu min nutfatin fa-izaa huwa khaseemum mubeen

78. Wa daraba lanaa maslanw-wa nasiya khalqahoo qaala mai-yuhyil'izaama wa hiya rameem

79. Qul yuh yeehal lazee ansha ahaaa awwala marrah; wa Huwa bikulli khalqin 'Aleem

80. Allazee ja'ala lakum minash shajaril akhdari naaran fa-izaaa antum minhu tooqidoon

81. Awa laisal lazee khalaqas samaawaati wal arda biqaadirin 'alaaa ai-yakhluqa mislahum; balaa wa Huwal Khallaaqul 'Aleem

82. Innamaa amruhooo izaaa araada shai'an ai-yaqoola lahoo kun fa-yakoon

83. Fa Subhaanal lazee biyadihee malakootu kulli shai-inw-wa ilaihi turja'oon

Surah Yaseen

يٰسٓ

Translation

1. Yâ-Sĩn.

2. By the Glorious Quran, rich in wisdom!

3. You ˹O Prophet˺ are truly one of the messengers

4. Upon the Straight Path.

5. ˹This is˺ a revelation from the Almighty, Most Merciful,

6. So that you may warn a people whose forefathers were not warned, and so are heedless.

7. The decree ˹of torment˺ has already been justified against most of them, for they will never believe.

8. ˹It is as if˺ we have put shackles around their necks up to their chins, so their heads are forced up,

9. And have placed a barrier before them and a barrier behind them and covered them ˹all˺ up, so they fail to see the truth.

10. It is the same whether you warn them or not—they will never believe.

11. You can only warn those who follow the Reminder1 and are in awe of the Most Compassionate without seeing Him.2 So give them the good news of forgiveness and an honorable reward.

12. It is certain we who resurrect the dead, and write what they send forth and what they leave behind. Everything is listed by us in a perfect Record.1

13. Give them an example ˹O Prophet˺ of the residents of a town, when the messengers came to them.

14. We sent them two messengers, but they rejected both. So we reinforced ˹the two˺ with a third, and they declared, "We have indeed been sent to you ˹as messengers˺."

15. The people replied, "You are only humans like us, and the Most Compassionate has not revealed anything. You are simply lying!"

16. The messengers responded, "Our Lord knows that we have truly been sent to you.

17. And our duty is only to deliver the message clearly."

18. The people replied, "We definitely see you as a bad omen for us. If you do not desist, we will certainly stone you to death and you will be touched with a painful punishment from us."

19. The messengers said, "Your bad omen lies within yourselves. Are you saying this because you are reminded ˹of the truth˺? In fact, you are a transgressing person."

20. Then from the farthest end of the city a man came, rushing. He advised, "O my people! Follow the messengers.

21. Follow those who ask no reward of you, and are ˹rightly˺ guided.

22. And why should I not worship the One who has originated me, and to whom you will be returned?

23. How could I take besides Him other gods whose intercession would not be of any benefit to me, nor could they save me if the Most Compassionate intended to harm me?

24. Indeed, I would then be clearly astray.

25. I do believe in your Lord, so listen to me."

26. ˹But they killed him, then˺ he was told ˹by the angels˺, "Enter Paradise!" He said, "If only my people knew

27. Of how my Lord has forgiven me, and made me one of the honorable."

28. We did not send any soldiers from the heavens against his people after his death, nor did we need to.

29. All it took was one ˹mighty˺ blast, and they were extinguished at once.

30. Oh pity, such beings! No messenger ever came to them without being mocked.

31. Have the deniers not considered how many peoples we destroyed before them who never came back to life again?

32. Yet they will all be brought before us.

33. There is a sign for them in the dead earth: We give it life, producing grain from it for them to eat.

34. And we have placed in it gardens of palm trees and grapevines, and caused springs to gush forth in it,

35. So that they may eat from its fruit, which they had no hand in making. Will they not then give thanks?

36. Glory be to the One Who created all things in pairs—ʿbe itʾ what the earth produces, their genders, or what they do not know!

37. There is also a sign for them in the night: We strip from it daylight, then—behold!—they are in darkness.

38. The sun travels for its fixed term. That is the design of the Almighty, All-Knowing.

39. As for the moon, we have ordained ʿpreciseʾ phases for it, until it ends up like an old, curved palm stalk.

40. It is not for the sun to catch up with the moon, 1 nor does the night outrun the day. Each is traveling in an orbit of its own.

41. Another sign for them is that we carried their ancestor's ʿwith Noahʾ in the fully loaded Ark,

42. And created for them similar things to ride in.

43. If we willed, we could drown them: then no one would respond to their cries, nor would they be rescued—

44. except by mercy from us, allowing them enjoyment for a ʿlittleʾ while.

45. ʿStill they turn awayʾ when it is said to them, "Beware of what is ahead of you ʿin the Hereafterʾ and what is behind you ʿof destroyed nationsʾ so you may be shown mercy."

46. Whenever a sign comes to them from their Lord, they turn away from it.

47. And when it is said to them, "Donate from what Allah has provided for you," the disbelievers say to the believers, "Why should we feed those whom Allah could have fed if He wanted to? You are clearly astray!"

48. And they ask ˹the believers˺, "When will this threat come to pass if what you say is true?"

49. They must be awaiting a single Blast, 1 which will seize them while they are ˹entrenched˺ in ˹worldly˺ disputes.

50. Then they will not be able to make a ˹last˺ will, nor can they return to their own people.

51. The Trumpet will be blown ˹a second time˺, then—behold!—they will rush from the graves to their Lord.

52. They will cry, "Woe to us! Who has raised us up from our place of rest? This must be what the Most Compassionate warned us of; the messengers told the truth!"

53. It will only take one Blast, then at once they will all be brought before us.

54. On that Day no soul will be wronged in the least, nor will you be rewarded except for what you used to do.

55. Indeed, on that Day the residents of Paradise will be busy enjoying themselves.

56. They and their spouses will be in ˹cool˺ shade, reclining on ˹canopied˺ couches.

57. There they will have fruits and whatever they desire.

58. And "Peace!" will be ˹their˺ greeting from the Merciful Lord.

59. ˹Then the disbelievers will be told,˺ "Step away ˹from the believers˺ this Day, O wicked ones!

60. Did I not command you, O Children of Adam, not to follow Satan, for he is truly your sworn enemy?

61. but to worship me ˹alone˺? This is the Straight Path.

62. Yet he already misled great multitudes of you. Did you not have any sense?

63. This is the Hell you were warned of.

64. Burn in it today for your disbelief."

65. On this Day We will seal their mouths, their hands will speak to us, and their feet will testify to what they used to commit.

66. Had we willed, we could have easily blinded their eyes, so they would struggle to find their way. How then could they see?

67. And had we willed, we could have transfigured them on the spot, 1 so they could neither progress forward nor turn back.

68. And whoever we grant a long life, we reverse them in development.1 Will they not then understand?

69. We have not taught him poetry, nor is it fitting for him. This ˹Book˺ is only a Reminder and a clear Quran

70. To warn whoever is ˹truly˺ alive and fulfill the decree ˹of torment˺ against the disbelievers.

71. Do they not see that we singlehandedly1 created for them, among other things, cattle that are under their control?

72. And we have subjected these ˹animals˺ to them, so they may ride some and eat others.

73. And they derive from them other benefits and drinks. Will they not then give thanks?

74. Still they have taken other gods besides Allah, hoping to be helped by them.

75. They cannot help the pagans, even though they serve the idols as dedicated guards.

76. So do not let their words grieve you ˹O Prophet˺. Indeed, we ˹fully˺ know what they conceal and what they reveal.

77. Do people not see that we have created them from a sperm drop, then—behold!—they openly challenge ˹Us˺?

78. And they argue with us—forgetting they were created—saying, "Who will give life to decayed bones?"

79. Say, ˹O Prophet,˺ "They will be revived by the One Who produced them the first time, for He has ˹perfect˺ knowledge of every created being.

80. ˹He is the One˺ Who gives you fire from green trees, and—behold!—you kindle ˹fire˺ from them

81. Can the One Who created the heavens and the earth not ˹easily˺ resurrect this ˹deniers˺?" Yes ˹He can˺! For He is the Master Creator, All-Knowing.

82. All it takes, when He wills something to be, is simply to say to it: "Be!" And it is!

83. So glory be to the One in Whose Hands is the authority over all things, and to whom ˹alone˺ you will ˹all˺ be returned.

Your notes:-

"The Heart of the Quran"

Surah
Ar-Rahman

الرحمن

Surah Ar-Rahman
الرحمن

The 55th portion of the Qur'an is known as Surah Ar-Rahman (Arabic text: الرحمان) meaning "The Beneficent," Numerous benefits and favors that Allah has conferred upon us are listed in this Surah. For example, the ayat "Fabi ayyi aalaaa'i Rabbikumaa tukazzibaan," repeated 31 times throughout the Surah, means "Then which of your Lord's blessings would you both deny?"

Muslims consider Surah ar Rahman to be significant in the Qur'an. By listening to Surah ar Rahman, hundreds of individuals have had their heart problems healed.

Surah ar Rahman contains a detailed list of all of Allah's benefits. The blessing in heaven has also been stated in addition to the benefit on earth.

Surah Ar-Rahman is the 55th chapter of the Quran, and it holds immense significance and importance in Islam. Here are some reasons why:

It emphasizes the Mercy of Allah: The title "Ar-Rahman" translates to "The Most Merciful," which highlights the emphasis on Allah's mercy and compassion. The chapter repeatedly mentions Allah's blessings and His mercy towards His creation, reminding Muslims of His infinite kindness and love.

It is a source of blessings: Muslims believe that reciting Surah Ar-Rahman brings numerous blessings and rewards from Allah. They believe that reciting it with sincerity and devotion can help them overcome difficulties, earn the mercy of Allah, and increase their faith.

It is a reminder of Allah's creation: Surah Ar-Rahman emphasizes the majesty and power of Allah's creation. It mentions the natural wonders of the universe, including the sun, the moon, and the stars, reminding Muslims of Allah's greatness and the intricate nature of His creation.

It emphasizes the importance of gratitude: The chapter emphasizes the importance of gratitude towards Allah for His blessings. It reminds Muslims of the many blessings they enjoy in life and encourages them to show appreciation and thankfulness towards Allah.

It is a call to action: Surah Ar-Rahman also contains a call to action for Muslims to reflect on Allah's blessings and mercy and to live a righteous life. It encourages them to act with kindness, compassion, and generosity towards others, as Allah has acted with mercy and kindness towards them.

In summary, Surah Ar-Rahman is a chapter of the Quran that emphasizes the mercy and compassion of Allah. Its significance lies in its reminder of Allah's creation, the importance of gratitude, and the call to action for Muslims to live a righteous life. It is a source of blessings and a powerful reminder of Allah's love and kindness towards His creation.

الرحمن
Surah Ar-Rahman

ٱلرَّحِيمِ ٱلرَّحْمَـٰنِ ٱللَّهِ بِسْمِ

﴿١﴾ ٱلرَّحْمَـٰنُ

﴿٢﴾ ٱلْقُرْءَانَ عَلَّمَ

﴿٣﴾ ٱلْإِنسَـٰنَ خَلَقَ

﴿٤﴾ ٱلْبَيَانَ عَلَّمَهُ

﴿٥﴾ بِحُسْبَانٍ وَٱلْقَمَرُ ٱلشَّمْسُ

﴿٦﴾ يَسْجُدَانِ وَٱلشَّجَرُ وَٱلنَّجْمُ

﴿٧﴾ ٱلْمِيزَانَ وَوَضَعَ رَفَعَهَا وَٱلسَّمَآءَ

﴿٨﴾ ٱلْمِيزَانِ فِى تَطْغَوْاْ أَلَّا

﴿٩﴾ ٱلْمِيزَانَ تُخْسِرُواْ وَلَا بِٱلْقِسْطِ ٱلْوَزْنَ وَأَقِيمُواْ

﴿١٠﴾ لِلْأَنَامِ وَضَعَهَا وَٱلْأَرْضَ

﴿١١﴾ ٱلْأَكْمَامِ ذَاتُ وَٱلنَّخْلُ فَٰكِهَةٌ فِيهَا

﴿١٢﴾ وَٱلرَّيْحَانُ ٱلْعَصْفِ ذُو وَٱلْحَبُّ

﴿١٣﴾ تُكَذِّبَانِ رَبِّكُمَا ءَالَآءِ فَبِأَىِّ

﴿١٤﴾ كَٱلْفَخَّارِ صَلْصَٰلٍ مِنَ ٱلْإِنسَٰنَ خَلَقَ

﴿١٥﴾ نَارٍ مِّن مَّارِجٍ مِنَ ٱلْجَآنَّ وَخَلَقَ

﴿١٦﴾ تُكَذِّبَانِ رَبِّكُمَا ءَالَآءِ فَبِأَىِّ

﴿١٧﴾ ٱلْمَغْرِبَيْنِ وَرَبُّ ٱلْمَشْرِقَيْنِ رَبُّ

﴿١٨﴾ تُكَذِّبَانِ رَبِّكُمَا ءَالَآءِ فَبِأَىِّ

﴿١٩﴾ يَلْتَقِيَانِ ٱلْبَحْرَيْنِ مَرَجَ

﴿٢٠﴾ يَبْغِيَانِ لَّا بَرْزَخٌ بَيْنَهُمَا

﴿٢١﴾ تُكَذِّبَانِ رَبِّكُمَا ءَالَآءِ فَبِأَىِّ

﴿٢٢﴾ وَٱلْمَرْجَانُ ٱللُّؤْلُؤُ مِنْهُمَا يَخْرُجُ

﴿٢٣﴾ تُكَذِّبَانِ رَبِّكُمَا ءَالَآءِ فَبِأَىِّ

﴿٢٤﴾ كَٱلْأَعْلَٰمِ ٱلْبَحْرِ فِى ٱلْمُنشَـَٔاتُ ٱلْجَوَارِ وَلَهُ

﴿٢٥﴾ تُكَذِّبَانِ رَبِّكُمَا ءَالَآءِ فَبِأَىِّ

﴿٢٦﴾ فَانٍ عَلَيْهَا مَنْ كُلُّ

﴿٢٧﴾ وَٱلْإِكْرَامِ ٱلْجَلَٰلِ ذُو رَبِّكَ وَجْهُ وَيَبْقَىٰ

﴿٢٨﴾ تُكَذِّبَانِ رَبِّكُمَا ءَالَآءِ فَبِأَىِّ

﴿٢٩﴾ شَأْنٍ فِى هُوَ يَوْمٍ كُلَّ ۚ وَٱلْأَرْضِ ٱلسَّمَٰوَٰتِ فِى مَن يَسْـَٔلُهُۥ

﴿٣٠﴾ تُكَذِّبَانِ رَبِّكُمَا ءَالَآءِ فَبِأَىِّ

﴿٣١﴾ ٱلثَّقَلَانِ أَيُّهَ لَكُمْ سَنَفْرُغُ

﴿٣٢﴾ تُكَذِّبَانِ رَبِّكُمَا ءَالَآءِ فَبِأَىِّ

ٱلسَّمَٰوَٰتِ أَقْطَارِ مِنْ تَنفُذُوا۟ أَن ٱسْتَطَعْتُمْ إِنِ وَٱلْإِنسِ ٱلْجِنِّ يَٰمَعْشَرَ
﴿٣٣﴾ بِسُلْطَٰنٍ إِلَّا تَنفُذُونَ لَا فَٱنفُذُوا۟ وَٱلْأَرْضِ

﴿٣٤﴾ تُكَذِّبَانِ رَبِّكُمَا ءَالَآءِ فَبِأَىِّ

﴿٣٥﴾ تَنتَصِرَانِ فَلَا وَنُحَاسٌ نَّارٍ مِّن شُوَاظٌ عَلَيْكُمَا يُرْسَلُ

﴿٣٦﴾ تُكَذِّبَانِ رَبِّكُمَا ءَالَآءِ فَبِأَىِّ

﴿٣٧﴾ كَٱلدِّهَانِ وَرْدَةً فَكَانَتِ ٱلسَّمَآءُ ٱنشَقَّتِ فَإِذَا

﴿٣٨﴾ تُكَذِّبَانِ رَبِّكُمَا ءَالَآءِ فَبِأَىِّ

﴿٣٩﴾ جَآنٌّ وَلَا إِنسٌ ذَنۢبِهِۦ عَن يُسْـَٔلُ لَّا فَيَوْمَئِذٍ

﴿٤٠﴾ تُكَذِّبَانِ رَبِّكُمَا ءَالَآءِ فَبِأَىِّ

﴿٤١﴾ وَٱلْأَقْدَامِ بِٱلنَّوَٰصِى فَيُؤْخَذُ بِسِيمَٰهُمُ ٱلْمُجْرِمُونَ يُعْرَفُ

﴿٤٢﴾ تُكَذِّبَانِ رَبِّكُمَا ءَالَآءِ فَبِأَىِّ

﴿٤٣﴾ ٱلْمُجْرِمُونَ بِهَا يُكَذِّبُ ٱلَّتِى جَهَنَّمُ هَٰذِهِۦ

﴿٤٤﴾ ءَانٍ حَمِيمٍ وَبَيْنَ بَيْنَهَا يَطُوفُونَ

﴿٤٥﴾ تُكَذِّبَانِ رَبِّكُمَا ءَالَآءِ فَبِأَىِّ

﴿٤٦﴾ جَنَّتَانِ رَبِّهِۦ مَقَامَ خَافَ وَلِمَنْ

﴿٤٧﴾ تُكَذِّبَانِ رَبِّكُمَا ءَالَآءِ فَبِأَىِّ

﴿٤٨﴾ أَفْنَانٍ ذَوَاتَآ

﴿٤٩﴾ تُكَذِّبَانِ رَبِّكُمَا ءَالَآءِ فَبِأَىِّ

﴿٥٠﴾ تَجْرِيَانِ عَيْنَانِ فِيهِمَا

﴿٥١﴾ تُكَذِّبَانِ رَبِّكُمَا ءَالَآءِ فَبِأَىِّ

﴿٥٢﴾ زَوْجَانِ فَٰكِهَةٍ كُلِّ مِن فِيهِمَا

﴿٥٣﴾ تُكَذِّبَانِ رَبِّكُمَا ءَالَآءِ فَبِأَىِّ

﴿٥٤﴾ دَانٍ ٱلْجَنَّتَيْنِ وَجَنَى ٱسْتَبْرَقٍ مِنْ بَطَآئِنُهَا فُرُشٍ عَلَىٰ مُتَّكِئِينَ

﴿٥٥﴾ تُكَذِّبَانِ رَبِّكُمَا ءَالَآءِ فَبِأَىِّ

﴿٥٦﴾ جَآنٌّ وَلَا قَبْلَهُمْ إِنسٌ يَطْمِثْهُنَّ لَمْ ٱلطَّرْفِ قَٰصِرَٰتُ فِيهِنَّ

﴿٥٧﴾ تُكَذِّبَانِ رَبِّكُمَا ءَالَآءِ فَبِأَىِّ

﴿٥٨﴾ وَٱلْمَرْجَانُ ٱلْيَاقُوتُ كَأَنَّهُنَّ

﴿٥٩﴾ تُكَذِّبَانِ رَبِّكُمَا ءَالَآءِ فَبِأَىِّ

﴿٦٠﴾ ٱلْإِحْسَـٰنُ إِلَّا ٱلْإِحْسَـٰنِ جَزَآءُ هَلْ

﴿٦١﴾ تُكَذِّبَانِ رَبِّكُمَا ءَالَآءِ فَبِأَىِّ

﴿٦٢﴾ جَنَّتَانِ دُونِهِمَا وَمِن

﴿٦٣﴾ تُكَذِّبَانِ رَبِّكُمَا ءَالَآءِ فَبِأَىِّ

﴿٦٤﴾ مُدْهَآمَّتَانِ

﴿٦٥﴾ تُكَذِّبَانِ رَبِّكُمَا ءَالَآءِ فَبِأَىِّ

﴿٦٦﴾ نَضَّاخَتَانِ عَيْنَانِ فِيهِمَا

﴿٦٧﴾ تُكَذِّبَانِ رَبِّكُمَا ءَالَآءِ فَبِأَىِّ

﴿٦٨﴾ وَرُمَّانٌ وَنَخْلٌ فَـٰكِهَةٌ فِيهِمَا

﴿٦٩﴾ تُكَذِّبَانِ رَبِّكُمَا ءَالَآءِ فَبِأَىِّ

﴿٧٠﴾ حِسَانٌ خَيْرَٰتٌ فِيهِنَّ

﴿٧١﴾ تُكَذِّبَانِ رَبِّكُمَا ءَالَآءِ فَبِأَىِّ

﴿٧٢﴾ ٱلْخِيَامِ فِى مَّقْصُورَٰتٌ حُورٌ

﴿٧٣﴾ تُكَذِّبَانِ رَبِّكُمَا ءَالَآءِ فَبِأَىِّ

﴿٧٤﴾ جَآنٌّ وَلَا قَبْلَهُمْ إِنسٌ يَطْمِثْهُنَّ لَمْ

﴿٧٥﴾ تُكَذِّبَانِ رَبِّكُمَا ءَالَآءِ فَبِأَىِّ

﴿٧٦﴾ حِسَانٍ وَعَبْقَرِىٍّ خُضْرٍ رَفْرَفٍ عَلَىٰ مُتَّكِئِينَ

﴿٧٧﴾ تُكَذِّبَانِ رَبِّكُمَا ءَالَآءِ فَبِأَىِّ

﴿٧٨﴾ وَٱلْإِكْرَامِ ٱلْجَلَٰلِ ذِى رَبِّكَ ٱسْمُ تَبَٰرَكَ

Your notes:-

"The Beneficent"

الرحمن

Surah Ar-Rahman

The Beneficent

الرَّحِيمِ الرَّحْمَـٰنِ اللَّهِ بِسْمِ

Bismillah hir rahman nir Raheem

In the name of Allah, the Entirely Merciful, the Especially Merciful

الرَّحْمَـٰنُ

Ar Rahmaan
(Allah) Most Gracious!

الْقُرْآنَ عَلَّمَ

Al-lamal Quran
It is He Who has taught the Qur´an.

الْإِنْسَانَ خَلَقَ

Khalaqal insaan
He has created man

الْبَيَانَ عَلَّمَهُ

Al-lamahul bayaan
He has taught him speech (and intelligence)

بِحُسْبَانٍ وَالْقَمَرُ الشَّمْسُ

Ashshamsu walqamaru bihusbaan
The sun and the moon follow courses (exactly) computed

يَسْجُدَانِ وَالشَّجَرُ وَالنَّجْمُ

Wannajmu washshajaru yasjudan
And the herbs and the trees – both (alike) prostrate in adoration

الْمِيزَانَ وَوَضَعَ رَفَعَهَا وَالسَّمَاءَ

Wassamaaa'a rafa'ahaa wa wada'al Meezan
And the Firmament has He raised high, and He has set up the Balance
(of Justice)

الْمِيزَانِ فِي تَطْغَوْا أَلَّا

Allaa tatghaw fil meezaan
In order that ye may not transgress (due) balance

الْمِيزَانَ تُخْسِرُوا وَلَا بِالْقِسْطِ الْوَزْنَ وَأَقِيمُوا

Wa aqeemul wazna bilqisti wa laa tukhsirul meezaan
So establish weight with justice and stay within the balance.

لِلْأَنَامِ وَضَعَهَا وَالْأَرْضَ

Wal arda wada'ahaa lilanaam
It is He Who has spread out the earth for (His) creatures

الْأَكْمَامِ ذَاتُ وَالنَّخْلُ فَاكِهَةٌ فِيهَا

Feehaa faakihatunw wan nakhlu zaatul akmaam

Therein is fruit and date palms, producing spathes (enclosing dates)

وَالرَّيْحَانُ الْعَصْفِ ذُو وَالْحَبُّ

Walhabbu zul 'asfi war Raihaan

Also, corn, with (its) leaves and stalk for fodder and sweet-smelling plants

تُكَذِّبَانِ رَبِّكُمَا آلَاءِ فَبِأَيِّ

Fabi ayyi aalaaa'i Rabbikumaa tukazzibaan

Then which of the favors of your Lord will ye deny?

كَالْفَخَّارِ صَلْصَالٍ مِنْ الْإِنْسَانَ خَلَقَ

Khalaqal insaana min salsaalin kalfakhkhaar

He created man from sounding clay like unto pottery

نَارٍ مِنْ مَارِجٍ مِنْ الْجَانَّ وَخَلَقَ

Wa khalaqal jaaan mim maarijim min naar

And He created Jinns from fire free of smoke

تُكَذِّبَانِ رَبِّكُمَا آلَاءِ فَبِأَيِّ

Fabi ayyi aalaaa'i Rabbikumaa tukazzibaan

Then which of the favors of your Lord will ye deny?

الْمَغْرِبَيْنِ وَرَبُّ الْمَشْرِقَيْنِ رَبُّ

Rabbul mashriqayni wa Rabbul maghribayn

(He is) Lord of the two Easts and Lord of the two Wests

تُكَذِّبَانِ رَبِّكُمَا آلَاءِ فَبِأَيِّ

Fabi ayyi aalaaa'i Rabbikumaa tukazzibaan
Then which of the favors of your Lord will ye deny?

يَلْتَقِيَانِ الْبَحْرَيْنِ مَرَجَ

Marajal bahrayni yalta qiyaan
He has let free the two bodies of flowing water, meeting together

يَبْغِيَانِ لَا بَرْزَخٌ بَيْنَهُمَا

Bainahumaa barzakhul laa yabghiyaan
Between them is a Barrier which they do not transgress

تُكَذِّبَانِ رَبِّكُمَا آلَاءِ فَبِأَيِّ

Fabi ayyi aalaaa'i Rabbikumaa tukazzibaan
Then which of the favors of your Lord will ye deny?

وَالْمَرْجَانُ اللُّؤْلُؤُ مِنْهُمَا يَخْرُجُ

Yakhruju minhumal lu 'lu u wal marjaan
Out of them come Pearls and Coral

تُكَذِّبَانِ رَبِّكُمَا آلَاءِ فَبِأَيِّ

Fabi ayyi aalaaa'i Rabbikumaa tukazzibaan
Then which of the favours of your Lord will ye deny?

كَالْأَعْلَامِ الْبَحْرِ فِي الْمُنْشَآتُ الْجَوَارِ وَلَهُ

Wa lahul jawaaril mun sha'aatu fil bahri kal a'laam
And his are the Ships sailing smoothly through the seas, lofty as mountains

تُكَذِّبَانِ رَبِّكُمَا آلَاءِ فَبِأَيِّ

Fabi ayyi aalaaa'i Rabbikumaa tukazzibaan.
Then which of the favors of your Lord will ye deny?

فَانٍ عَلَيْهَا مَنْ كُلُّ

Kullu man 'alaihaa faan
All that is on earth will perish

وَالْإِكْرَامِ الْجَلَالِ ذُو رَبِّكَ وَجْهُ وَيَبْقَى

Wa yabqaa wajhu rabbika zul jalaali wal ikraam
But will abide (forever) the Face of thy Lord, full of Majesty, Bounty,
and Honour

تُكَذِّبَانِ رَبِّكُمَا آلَاءِ فَبِأَيِّ

Fabi ayyi aalaaa'i Rabbikumaa tukazzibaan
Then which of the favours of your Lord will ye deny?

شَأْنٍ فِي هُوَ يَوْمٍ كُلَّ وَالْأَرْضِ السَّمَاوَاتِ فِي مَنْ يَسْأَلُهُ

Yas'aluhoo man fissamaawaati walard; kulla yawmin huwa fee shaan
Of Him seeks (its need) every creature in the heavens and on earth:
every day in (new) Splendour doth He (shine)!

تُكَذِّبَانِ رَبِّكُمَا آلَاءِ فَبِأَيِّ

Fabi ayyi aalaaa'i Rabbikumaa tukazzibaan
Then which of the favours of your Lord will ye deny?

الثَّقَلَانِ أَيُّهَ لَكُمْ سَنَفْرُغُ

Sanafrughu lakum ayyuhas saqalaan
Soon shall we settle your affairs, O both ye worlds!

تُكَذِّبَانِ رَبِّكُمَا آلَاءِ فَبِأَيِّ

Fabi ayyi aalaaa'i Rabbikumaa tukazzibaan.
Then which of the favors of your Lord will ye deny?

السَّمَاوَاتِ أَقْطَارِ مِنْ تَنْفُذُوا أَنْ اسْتَطَعْتُمْ إِنِ وَالْإِنْسِ الْجِنِّ مَعْشَرَ يَا
بِسُلْطَانٍ إِلَّا تَنْفُذُونَ لَا فَانْفُذُوا وَالْأَرْضِ

Yaa ma'sharal jinni wal insi inis tata'tum an tanfuzoo min aqtaaris
samaawaati wal ardi fanfuzoo; laa tanfuzoona illaa bisultaan
O ye assembly of Jinns and men! If it be ye can pass beyond the zones
of the heavens and the earth, pass ye! Not without authority shall ye
be able to pass!

تُكَذِّبَانِ رَبِّكُمَا آلَاءِ فَبِأَيِّ

Fabi ayyi aalaaa'i Rabbikumaa tukazzibaan.
Then which of the favors of your Lord will ye deny?

تَنْتَصِرَانِ فَلَا وَنُحَاسٌ نَارٍ مِنْ شُوَاظٌ عَلَيْكُمَا يُرْسَلُ

Yursalu 'alaikumaa shuwaazum min naarinw-wa nuhaasun falaa
tantasiraan
On you will be sent (O ye evil one's twain!) a flame of fire (to burn)
and a smoke (to choke): no defence will ye have

تُكَذِّبَانِ رَبِّكُمَا آلَاءِ فَبِأَيِّ

Fabi ayyi aalaaa'i Rabbikumaa tukazzibaan.
Then which of the favors of your Lord will ye deny?

كَالدِّهَانِ وَرْدَةً فَكَانَتِ السَّمَاءُ انْشَقَّتِ فَإِذَا

Fa-izan shaqqatis samaaa'u fakaanat wardatan kaddihaan

When the sky is rent asunder, and it becomes red like ointment

تُكَذِّبَانِ رَبِّكُمَا آلَاءِ فَبِأَيِّ

Fabi ayyi aalaaa'i Rabbikumaa tukazzibaan.

Then which of the favors of your Lord will ye deny?

جَانٌّ وَلَا إِنْسٌ ذَنْبِهِ عَنْ يُسْأَلُ لَا فَيَوْمَئِذٍ

Fa-yawma'izil laa yus'alu 'an zambiheee insunw wa laa jaann

On that Day, no question will be asked of man or Jinn about his sin.

تُكَذِّبَانِ رَبِّكُمَا آلَاءِ فَبِأَيِّ

Fabi ayyi aalaaa'i Rabbikumaa tukazzibaan.

Then which of the favors of your Lord will ye deny?

وَالْأَقْدَامِ بِالنَّوَاصِي فَيُؤْخَذُ بِسِيمَاهُمْ الْمُجْرِمُونَ يُعْرَفُ

Yu'raful mujrimoona biseemaahum fa'yu'khazu binna waasi wal aqdaam

(For) the sinners will be known by their marks: their forelocks and feet will seize them

تُكَذِّبَانِ رَبِّكُمَا آلَاءِ فَبِأَيِّ

Fabi ayyi aalaaa'i Rabbikumaa tukazzibaan

Then which of the favours of your Lord will ye deny?

الْمُجْرِمُونَ بِهَا يُكَذِّبُ الَّتِي جَهَنَّمُ هَـٰذِهِ

Haazihee jahannamul latee yukazzibu bihal mujrimoon

This is the Hell that the Sinners deny

آنٍ حَمِيمٍ وَبَيْنَ بَيْنَهَا يَطُوفُونَ

Yatoofoona bainahaa wa baina hameemim aan
They will wander around in its midst and the midst of boiling hot water!

تُكَذِّبَانِ رَبِّكُمَا آلَاءِ فَبِأَيِّ

Fabi ayyi aalaaa'i Rabbikumaa tukazzibaan
Then which of the favours of your Lord will ye deny?

جَنَّتَانِ رَبِّهِ مَقَامَ خَافَ وَلِمَنْ

Wa liman khaafa maqaama rabbihee jannataan
But for such as fear the time when they will stand before (the Judgment Seat of) their Lord, there will be two Gardens

تُكَذِّبَانِ رَبِّكُمَا آلَاءِ فَبِأَيِّ

Fabi ayyi aalaaa'i Rabbikumaa tukazzibaan
Then which of the favours of your Lord will ye deny?

أَفْنَانٍ ذَوَاتَا

Zawaataaa afnaan
Containing all kinds (of trees and delights)

تُكَذِّبَانِ رَبِّكُمَا آلَاءِ فَبِأَيِّ

Fabi ayyi aalaaa'i Rabbikumaa tukazzibaan
Then which of the favours of your Lord will ye deny?

تَجْرِيَانِ عَيْنَانِ فِيهِمَا

Feehimaa 'aynaani tajriyaan

In them (each) will be two springs flowing (free)

تُكَذِّبَانِ رَبِّكُمَا آلَاءِ فَبِأَيِّ

Fabi ayyi aalaaa'i Rabbikumaa tukazzibaan

Then which of the favours of your Lord will ye deny?

زَوْجَانِ فَاكِهَةٍ كُلَّ مِنْ فِيهِمَا

Feehimaa min kulli faakihatin zawjaan

In them will be Fruits of every kind, two and two

تُكَذِّبَانِ رَبِّكُمَا آلَاءِ فَبِأَيِّ

Fabi ayyi aalaaa'i Rabbikumaa tukazzibaan

Then which of the favours of your Lord will ye deny?

دَانِ الْجَنَّتَيْنِ وَجَنَى إِسْتَبْرَقٍ مِنْ بَطَائِنُهَا فُرُشٍ عَلَىٰ مُتَّكِئِينَ

Muttaki'eena 'alaa furushim bataaa'inuhaa min istabraq; wajanal jannataini daan

They will recline on Carpets, whose inner linings will be rich brocade: the Fruit of the Gardens will be near (and easy to reach).

تُكَذِّبَانِ رَبِّكُمَا آلَاءِ فَبِأَيِّ

Fabi ayyi aalaaa'i Rabbikumaa tukazzibaan

Then which of the favours of your Lord will ye deny?

جَانٌّ وَلَا قَبْلَهُمْ إِنْسٌ يَطْمِثْهُنَّ لَمْ الطَّرْفِ قَاصِرَاتُ فِيهِنَّ

Feehinna qaasiratut tarfi lam yatmishunna insun qablahum wa laa jaaann

In them will be (Maidens), chaste, restraining their glances, whom no man or Jinn before them has touched

تُكَذِّبَانِ رَبِّكُمَا آلَاءِ فَبِأَيِّ

Fabi ayyi aalaaa'i Rabbikumaa tukazzibaan
Then which of the favours of your Lord will ye deny?

وَالْمَرْجَانُ الْيَاقُوتُ كَأَنَّهُنَّ

Ka annahunnal yaaqootu wal marjaan
Like unto Rubies and coral.

تُكَذِّبَانِ رَبِّكُمَا آلَاءِ فَبِأَيِّ

Fabi ayyi aalaaa'i Rabbikumaa tukazzibaan
Then which of the favours of your Lord will ye deny?

الْإِحْسَانُ إِلَّا الْإِحْسَانِ جَزَاءُ هَلْ

Hal jazaaa'ul ihsaani illal ihsaan
Is there any Reward for Good – other than Good?

تُكَذِّبَانِ رَبِّكُمَا آلَاءِ فَبِأَيِّ

Fabi ayyi aalaaa'i Rabbikumaa tukazzibaan
Then which of the favours of your Lord will ye deny?

جَنَّتَانِ دُونِهِمَا وَمِنْ

Wa min doonihimaa jannataan
And besides these two, there are two other Gardens

تُكَذِّبَانِ رَبِّكُمَا آلَاءِ فَبِأَيِّ

Fabi ayyi aalaaa'i Rabbikumaa tukazzibaan
Then which of the favours of your Lord will ye deny?

مُدْهَامَّتَانِ

Mudhaaammataan
Dark green in color (from plentiful watering)

تُكَذِّبَانِ رَبِّكُمَا آلَاءِ فَبِأَيِّ

Fabi ayyi aalaaa'i Rabbikumaa tukazzibaan
Then which of the favours of your Lord will ye deny?

نَضَّاخَتَانِ عَيْنَانِ فِيهِمَا

Feehimaa 'aynaani nad daakhataan
In them (each) will be two springs pouring forth water in continuous abundance

تُكَذِّبَانِ رَبِّكُمَا آلَاءِ فَبِأَيِّ

Fabi ayyi aalaaa'i Rabbikumaa tukazzibaan
Then which of the favours of your Lord will ye deny?

وَرُمَّانٌ وَنَخْلٌ فَاكِهَةٌ فِيهِمَا

Feehimaa faakihatunw wa nakhlunw wa rummaan
In them will be Fruits, dates, and pomegranates

تُكَذِّبَانِ رَبِّكُمَا آلَاءِ فَبِأَيِّ

Fabi ayyi aalaaa'i Rabbikumaa tukazzibaan
Then which of the favours of your Lord will ye deny?

حِسَانٌ خَيْرَاتٌ فِيهِنَّ

Feehinna khairaatun hisaan
In them will be fair (Companions), reasonable, beautiful

تُكَذِّبَانِ رَبِّكُمَا آلَاءِ فَبِأَيِّ

Fabi ayyi aalaaa'i Rabbikumaa tukazzibaan
Then which of the favours of your Lord will ye deny?

الْخِيَامِ فِي مَقْصُورَاتٌ حُورٌ

Hoorum maqsooraatun fil khiyaam
Companions restrained (as to their glances) in (goodly) pavilions

تُكَذِّبَانِ رَبِّكُمَا آلَاءِ فَبِأَيِّ

Fabi ayyi aalaaa'i Rabbikumaa tukazzibaan
Then which of the favours of your Lord will ye deny?

جَانٌّ وَلَا قَبْلَهُمْ إِنْسٌ يَطْمِثْهُنَّ لَمْ

Lam yatmis hunna insun qablahum wa laa jaaann
Whom no man or Jinn before them has touched

تُكَذِّبَانِ رَبِّكُمَا آلَاءِ فَبِأَيِّ

Fabi ayyi aalaaa'i Rabbikumaa tukazzibaan
Then which of the favours of your Lord will ye deny?

حِسَانٍ وَعَبْقَرِيٍّ خُضْرٍ رَفْرَفٍ عَلَىٰ مُتَّكِئِينَ

Muttaki'eena 'alaa rafrafin khudrinw wa 'abqariyyin hisaan
Reclining on green Cushions and rich Carpets of beauty.

تُكَذِّبَانِ رَبِّكُمَا آلَاءِ فَبِأَيِّ

Fabi ayyi aalaaa'i Rabbikumaa tukazzibaan

Then which of the favours of your Lord will ye deny?

وَالْإِكْرَامِ الْجَلَالِ ذِي رَبِّكَ اسْمُ تَبَارَكَ

Tabaarakasmu Rabbika Zil-Jalaali wal-Ikraam

Blessed be the name of thy Lord, full of Majesty, Bounty, and Honour.

Your notes:-

"The Beneficent"

Surah Ar-Rahman

Pronunciation

1. Ar Rahmaan

2. Al-lamal Quran

3. Khalaqal insaan

4. Al-lamahul bayaan

5. Ashshamsu walqamaru bihusbaan

6. Wannajmu washshajaru yasjudan

7. Wassamaaa'a rafa'ahaa wa wada'al Meezan

8. Allaa tatghaw fil meezaan

9. Wa aqeemul wazna bilqisti wa laa tukhsirul meezaan

10. Wal arda wada'ahaa lilanaam

11. Feehaa faakihatunw wan nakhlu zaatul akmaam

12. Walhabbu zul 'asfi war Raihaan

13. Fabi ayyi aalaaa'i Rabbikumaa tukazzibaan

14. Khalaqal insaana min salsaalin kalfakhkhaar

15. Wa khalaqal jaaan mim maarijim min naar

16. Fabi ayyi aalaaa'i Rabbikumaa tukazzibaan

17. Rabbul mashriqayni wa Rabbul maghribayn

18. Fabi ayyi aalaaa'i Rabbikumaa tukazzibaan

19. Marajal bahrayni yalta qiyaan

20. Bainahumaa barzakhul laa yabghiyaan

21. Fabi ayyi aalaaa'i Rabbikumaa tukazzibaan

22. Yakhruju minhumal lu 'lu u wal marjaan

23. Fabi ayyi aalaaa'i Rabbikumaa tukazzibaan

24. Wa lahul jawaaril mun sha'aatu fil bahri kal a'laam

25. Fabi ayyi aalaaa'i Rabbikumaa tukazzibaan.

26. Kullu man 'alaihaa faan

27. Wa yabqaa wajhu rabbika zul jalaali wal ikraam

28. Fabi ayyi aalaaa'i Rabbikumaa tukazzibaan.

29. Yas'aluhoo man fissamaawaati walard; kulla yawmin huwa fee shaan

30. Fabi ayyi aalaaa'i Rabbikumaa tukazzibaan.

31. Sanafrughu lakum ayyuhas saqalaan

32. Fabi ayyi aalaaa'i Rabbikumaa tukazzibaan.

33. Yaa ma'sharal jinni wal insi inis tata'tum an tanfuzoo min aqtaaris samaawaati wal ardi fanfuzoo; laa tanfuzoona illaa bisultaan

34. Fabi ayyi aalaaa'i Rabbikumaa tukazzibaan.

35. Yursalu 'alaikumaa shuwaazum min naarinw-wa nuhaasun falaa tantasiraan

36. Fabi ayyi aalaaa'i Rabbikumaa tukazzibaan.

37. Fa-izan shaqqatis samaaa'u fakaanat wardatan kaddihaan

38. Fabi ayyi aalaaa'i Rabbikumaa tukazzibaan.

39. Fa-yawma'izil laa yus'alu 'an zambiheee insunw wa laa jaann

40. Fabi ayyi aalaaa'i Rabbikumaa tukazzibaan.

41. Yu'raful mujrimoona biseemaahum fa'yu'khazu binna waasi wal aqdaam

42. Fabi ayyi aalaaa'i Rabbikumaa tukazzibaan.

43. Haazihee jahannamul latee yukazzibu bihal mujrimoon

44. Yatoofoona bainahaa wa baina hameemim aan

45. Fabi ayyi aalaaa'i Rabbikumaa tukazzibaan.

46. Wa liman khaafa maqaama rabbihee jannataan

47. Fabi ayyi aalaaa'i Rabbikumaa tukazzibaan.

48. Zawaataaa afnaan

49. Fabi ayyi aalaaa'i Rabbikumaa tukazzibaan.

50. Feehimaa 'aynaani tajriyaan

51. Fabi ayyi aalaaa'i Rabbikumaa tukazzibaan.

52. Feehimaa min kulli faakihatin zawjaan

53. Fabi ayyi aalaaa'i Rabbikumaa tukazzibaan.

54. Muttaki'eena 'alaa furushim bataaa'inuhaa min istabraq; wajanal jannataini daan

55. Fabi ayyi aalaaa'i Rabbikumaa tukazzibaan.

56. Feehinna qaasiratut tarfi lam yatmishunna insun qablahum wa laa jaaann

57. Fabi ayyi aalaaa'i Rabbikumaa tukazzibaan.

58. Ka annahunnal yaaqootu wal marjaan

59. Fabi ayyi aalaaa'i Rabbikumaa tukazzibaan.

60. Hal jazaaa'ul ihsaani illal ihsaan

61. Fabi ayyi aalaaa'i Rabbikumaa tukazzibaan.

62. Wa min doonihimaa jannataan

63. Fabi ayyi aalaaa'i Rabbikumaa tukazzibaan.

64. Mudhaaammataan

65. Fabi ayyi aalaaa'i Rabbikumaa tukazzibaan.

66. Feehimaa 'aynaani nad daakhataan

67. Fabi ayyi aalaaa'i Rabbikumaa tukazzibaan.

68. Feehimaa faakihatunw wa nakhlunw wa rummaan

69. Fabi ayyi aalaaa'i Rabbikumaa tukazzibaan.

70. Feehinna khairaatun hisaan

71. Fabi ayyi aalaaa'i Rabbikumaa tukazzibaan.

72. Hoorum maqsooraatun fil khiyaam

73. Fabi ayyi aalaaa'i Rabbikumaa tukazzibaan.

74. Lam yatmis hunna insun qablahum wa laa jaaann

75. Fabi ayyi aalaaa'i Rabbikumaa tukazzibaan.

76. Muttaki'eena 'alaa rafrafin khudrinw wa 'abqariyyin hisaan

77. Fabi ayyi aalaaa'i Rabbikumaa tukazzibaan.

78. Tabaarakasmu Rabbika Zil-Jalaali wal-Ikraam

Your notes:-

"The Beneficent"

Surah Ar-Rahman

Translation

1. (Allah) Most Gracious!

2. It is He Who has taught the Qur´an.

3. He has created man:

4. He has taught him speech (and intelligence).

5. The sun and the moon follow courses (exactly) computed;

6. And the herbs and the trees – both (alike) prostrate in adoration.

7. And the Firmament has He raised high, and He has set up the Balance (of Justice),

8. In order that ye may not transgress (due) balance.

9. So establish weight with justice and stay within the balance.

10. It is He Who has spread out the earth for (His) creatures:

11. Therein is fruit and date palms, producing spathes (enclosing dates);

12. Also, corn, with (its) leaves and stalk for fodder, and sweet-smelling plants.

13. Then which of the favors of your Lord will ye deny?

14. He created man from sounding clay like pottery,

15. And He created Jinns from fire free of smoke:

16. Then which of the favors of your Lord will ye deny?

17. (He is) Lord of the two Easts and Lord of the two Wests:

18. Then which of the favors of your Lord will ye deny?

19. He has let free the two bodies of flowing water, meeting together:

20. Between them is a Barrier which they do not transgress:

21. Then which of the favors of your Lord will ye deny?

22. Out of them come Pearls and Coral:

23. Then which of the favors of your Lord will ye deny?

24. And his are the Ships sailing smoothly through the seas, lofty as mountains:

25. Then which of the favors of your Lord will ye deny?

26. All that is on earth will perish:

27. But will abide (forever) the Face of thy Lord, full of Majesty, Bounty, and Honour.

28. Then which of the favors of your Lord will ye deny?

29. Of Him seeks (its need) every creature in the heavens and on earth: every day in (new) Splendour doth He (shine)!

30. Then which of the favors of your Lord will ye deny?

31. Soon shall we settle your affairs, O both ye worlds!

32. Then which of the favors of your Lord will ye deny?

33. O ye assembly of Jinns and men! If it be ye can pass beyond the zones of the heavens and the earth, pass you! Not without authority shall ye be able to pass!

34. Then which of the favors of your Lord will ye deny?

35. On you will be sent (O ye evil one's twain!) a flame of fire (to burn) and a smoke (to choke): no defense will ye have:

36. Then which of the favors of your Lord will ye deny?

37. When the sky is rent asunder, and it becomes red like ointment:

38. Then which of the favors of your Lord will ye deny?

39. On that Day, no question will be asked of man or Jinn about his sin.

40. Then which of the favors of your Lord will ye deny?

41. (For) the sinners will be known by their marks: their forelocks and feet will seize them.

42. Then which of the favors of your Lord will ye deny?

43. This is the Hell that the Sinners deny:

44. They will wander around in its midst and the midst of boiling hot water!

45. Then which of the favors of your Lord will ye deny?

46. But for such as fear the time when they will stand before (the Judgment Seat of) their Lord, there will be two Gardens-

47. Then which of the favors of your Lord will ye deny?

48. Containing all kinds (of trees and delights);-

49. Then which of the favors of your Lord will ye deny?

50. In them (each) will be two springs flowing (free);

51. Then which of the favors of your Lord will ye deny?

52. In them will be Fruits of every kind, two and two.

53. Then which of the favors of your Lord will ye deny?

54. They will recline on Carpets, whose inner linings will be rich brocade: the Fruit of the Gardens will be near (and easy to reach).

55. Then which of the favors of your Lord will ye deny?

56. In them will be (Maidens), chaste, restraining their glances, whom no man or Jinn before them has touched;

57. Then which of the favors of your Lord will ye deny?

58. Like unto Rubies and coral.

59. Then which of the favors of your Lord will ye deny?

60. Is there any Reward for Good – other than Good?

61. Then which of the favors of your Lord will ye deny?

62. And besides these two, there are two other Gardens-

63. Then which of the favors of your Lord will ye deny?

64. Dark green in color (from plentiful watering).

65. Then which of the favors of your Lord will ye deny?

66. In them (each) will be two springs pouring forth water in continuous abundance:

67. Then which of the favors of your Lord will ye deny?

68. In them will be Fruits, dates, and pomegranates:

69. Then which of the favors of your Lord will ye deny?

70. In them will be fair (Companions), reasonable, beautiful;

71. Then which of the favors of your Lord will ye deny?

72. Companions restrained (as to their glances) in (goodly) pavilions

73. Then which of the favors of your Lord will ye deny?

74. Whom no man or Jinn before them has touched

75. Then which of the favors of your Lord will ye deny?

76. Reclining on green Cushions and rich Carpets of beauty.

77. Then which of the favors of your Lord will ye deny?

78. Blessed be the name of thy Lord, full of Majesty, Bounty, and Honour.

Your notes:-

"The Beneficent"

Printed in Great Britain
by Amazon

33897558R00055